Weston-super-Mare
REUNITED

SHARON POOLE

HALSGROVE

First published in Great Britain in 2010

British Library Cataloguing-in-Publication Data
A CIP record for this title is available from the British Library

ISBN 978 0 85704 016 9

HALSGROVE
Halsgrove House,
Ryelands Industrial Estate,
Bagley Road, Wellington, Somerset TA21 9PZ
Tel: 01823 653777   Fax: 01823 216796
email: sales@halsgrove.com

Part of the Halsgrove group of companies
Information on all Halsgrove titles is available at: www.halsgrove.com

Printed and bound in Great Britain by SRP Ltd., Exeter

Contents

Acknowledgements

As usual, I am indebted to the many people that have kindly lent me photographs and memorabilia, as well as provided information. Without their assistance there would be no book. I have made every effort to be accurate with information and names, and apologise for any omissions or errors. I would particularly like to thank the following :-

Brian Austin	R. Ellis	David Kidd
Mrs Batchelor	Mrs Gwen Ellis	Alan Merrick
Derek Boardman	Ann Fewings	Jean Overy
Christine Bowen	Hilda Goold	Jane Paterson
Rod Brenner	Margaret Harvey	Alan Richardson
Carole Bressington	John Hess	Sara Stock
Mrs Burrows	E. F. Hooper	Joe Thomas
Marina Coles	Jeff Hynds	Mr and Mrs Tottle
Yvonne Cresswell	Pat Johnson	Mrs Venn
The Late Eileen and	Jane Johnstone	Doris Wilsher
Laurie Crews	Mrs Pat Jones	Carol White
Margaret Drury	The Late Mrs Jones	

Introduction

This book is one in a new series by publishers Halsgrove, celebrating the activities and achievements of the people of Weston-super-Mare over the last seventy years. Using a wide range of photographs of people, events, groups, and sports teams, the book has been produced in an album style and it is my hope that the images will stir memories and truly "reunite" Westonians old and young, past and present.

Weston-super-Mare, like every place, large or small, is the product of its people. Some may become famous but the majority will only be known to family, friends and the local community. The contribution of these people to the health, wealth and happiness of the town is immense and often goes unknown and unmarked and in a small way I hope to remedy that situation with this book.

People chose to settle in this south-west corner of the country in the Bronze Age around 4000 years ago, when nomadic herders took the decision to settle down and farm on the hillside and fertile levels. The population gradually grew and by medieval times, the village of Weston had considerable importance and wealth. This was enhanced further when the concept of the Seaside Holiday took off at the end of the eighteenth century and canny locals were quick to cash in on the opportunities afforded by the presence of wealthy visitors. The arrival of Brunel's Bristol & Exeter Railway in 1841 put the seal on the town's popularity as a resort. Between 1811 and 1901 the resident population grew from 163 to nearly 20,000. Today it is closer to 70,000.

The last 70 years have seen the construction of some of the town's most iconic and memorable landmarks, among them the Open Air Swimming Pool, with its distinctive diving boards and the Grand Pier Pavilion, built to replace the original one which was destroyed by fire. They have also seen their loss, to closure and planned demolition and fire respectively.

Weston is now well into the new millennium facing yet further challenges. Many of the town's major employers have closed or moved factory bases, notably the helicopter manufacturer Westlands and Clarks' Shoe factory. There have also been new trends in tourism, with foreign shores becoming the destination of choice, instead of Weston's three miles of golden sands. This has seen a huge reduction in the number of hotels and guest houses as they fall victim to economic pressures. But the town is also growing and changing in other ways.

Weston has seen its share of immigrants, from the Romans in the fifth century and the German miners in the sixteenth century right through to the Italian, Jewish and Belgian refugees from the two World Wars and the present day Poles, Russians, Asians, Chinese and Greek Cypriots, to name just a few. All have enriched the life and culture of Weston and created a vibrant and lively town.

As for Weston's future – we can but wait and see. The economic crisis has meant the closure of many shops and businesses. Conversely, it may also help to revive British tourism as more people opt to holiday in their own country.

I hope you enjoy reminiscing as you browse the images. You may even recognise yourself, your relations or friends in some of these photographs.

The 1930s

The 1930s are remembered nationally as the period of the Great Depression, when unemployment doubled to 2.5 million as demand for British products collapsed, leaving some families virtually destitute.

With few manufacturing industries, which bore the brunt of the downtown, Weston-super-Mare was not as badly hit as northern towns and resorts. In fact, this ten year period was one of the most dynamic in Weston's history. Many well-known buildings were constructed at this time, among them the Odeon Cinema, Open Air Pool, Rozel Bandstand and Weston Grammar School. Popular music really took off around this time as radios became commonplace in the home. Bands were booming and dancing was never more popular. There were ballrooms at the Winter Gardens, the Grand Atlantic Hotel and even the new Grand Pier Pavilion.

The 1930s saw a huge growth in house-building. More than four million homes were built nationally between 1919 and 1939 and Weston's population grew by 30% in just ten years. Most of the new property in Weston was being built at Milton, then on the outskirts of the town in the green belt between Weston and Worle. With building societies eager to offer mortgages to a wider range of people, home ownership at last became feasible for more working people. A new detached house with three bedrooms and two reception rooms in Stanhope Road on the Uphill Park Estate was on sale for £950. The introduction of hire purchase meant people could equip their homes with the latest gadgets. The increasing opportunities for employment and variety of housing choices brought many new people into the town and with them came new facilities and services as well as new ideas and expectations.

In 1935 the country celebrated the Golden Jubilee of King George V and Queen Mary. Among other events, Weston organised a Thanksgiving Service in Grove Park, a balloon release and a Pageant of Empire at Knightstone Theatre.

In 1936 Western Airways began operating scheduled air services from Weston Airport. These became so popular that after the first weekend of operation the Weston Mercury reported that additional air liners had to be brought in to cope with the numbers. It was a short flight across the Bristol Channel to and from Wales, a journey particularly popular with the Welsh miners on a Sunday when the sale of alcohol was banned in their country! So popular in fact that by 1938 the service was half-hourly! There were also occasional flights to and from Paris.

1937 was Coronation year for George VI and Queen Elizabeth. As increased motor transport in the form of both private cars and public buses arrived, so the end followed for the trams which stopped running on 17 April 1937. The same year Weston was granted Borough status and local entrepreneur and businessman Henry Butt was installed as the first Mayor in a ceremony watched by hundreds in Grove Park.

In September 1939 the Second World War broke out and life changed yet again. The airport was requisitioned by the Air Ministry as a reserve centre and the pleasure steamers that plied up and down the channel between Birnbeck Pier and other resorts were seized for minesweeping duties. Parks and gardens would become part of the Dig for Victory campaign and the bright lights of this happy family resort would be dimmed for the foreseeable future. The interwar years were arguably Weston's golden era and saw the most investment in the town than in any other period. Much of it was funded with public money, a far cry from today's reliance on partnerships and the private sector. For their part residents got a wide range of attractions and services, built and run by the town for the town.

Beach Road Bus Station Café, c.1938. The Bus Station was built in 1928 on a site once occupied by Belvedere, one of the earliest seafront villas. The ground floor housed the bus garage, ticket office and information desk with this café on the first floor offering a superb view over the Beach Lawns to the sea. Because of its convenient location, it was a popular meeting place, especially for romantic liaisons! The Bus Station was demolished in 1988, after de-regulation of bus services two years earlier, and the site sold for re-development. Carlton Mansions and Birnbeck Court sheltered housing now occupy the site.

William Meakin with his daughter Gwen, pictured outside his cycle shop and sweet shop and tobacconists at 38 - 40 Baker Street, 1935. Meakin took over the cycle repairs shop in 1925. The sweet shop was originally run by his sister Frances, and then later by his daughter Gwen. In 1932 he also purchased the old stables and yard next door. When the Second World War broke out, Meakin won a government contract to empty requisitioned houses. After the War, this developed into a house-removal business and later expanded yet again into second-hand furniture and "antiques". This was continued by Meakin's son, also called William. William junior retired in October 1987 and the business closed. The premises were demolished in 2004 and the site has been redeveloped with housing association flats.

William Meakin outside his Baker Street premises, c.1938.

Doris Allen on Weston Sands, c.1932. Doris was born in Shepton Mallet and came to Weston with her family, as a young girl. As soon as she was old enough she worked at one of the tea stalls on the beach, close to the entrance to the Grand Pier. It was there she met her future husband George Boardman. They were married at Emmanuel Church in 1936 and later had two children, Derek and Margaret. In 1940 George enlisted in the Somerset Light Infantry. During his army service he caught tuberculosis which resulted in his early death, shortly after his return to their home in Bridge Road at the end of the Second World War. Their children still live in Weston.

George Boardman in one of the "Auto Skooters", a forerunner of the dodgem car, on the Grand Pier at Weston, 1935. George came to Weston from Liverpool a couple of years earlier in search of work. It was the height of the Great Depression, the effects of which were felt much harder in the industrial cities in the north of England. He had no money, but managed to survive on the casual work he picked up along the way. Once in Weston-super-Mare he got a job on the pier maintaining the rides. It was during this time that he met Doris Allen. In the winter months, he worked as a builder's labourer, returning to the pier every summer season.

Al Lever and his dance orchestra at the Winter Gardens Pavilion, c.1938. The Winter Gardens employed a resident orchestra for each summer season. Al Lever was a well known band leader, and several of his musicians went on to form their own bands, including Joe Loss, who by the end of the 1930s was the biggest name in the Big Band world. Vera Lynn gave her first ever radio broadcast with him in 1937. Loss and his band continued playing until the 1980s.

Henry Butt, first Mayor of Weston Borough Council in the new mayoral robes.
Weston was granted borough status at a Charter Ceremony in Grove Park in 1937.
Butt was a local entrepreneur with an interest in a wide range of businesses. He had
come to the town as a young man, from Langport in Somerset. When he eventually
bought a house at 1 Eastfield Park he named it Langport Villa. He began working
for a local coal merchant, but had soon hired a horse and cart and set up as a carrier.
By the start of the First World War he had made enough to purchase Milton Quarry
and set about expanding and modernising it. By the 1930s he was buying up
Victorian villas on the hillside. With servants now a rarity reserved for the wealthy
few, these homes had become too large for single families. Butt began to convert
them into "modern" mansion flats. Now a millionaire, he was instrumental in raising
funds to build the new hospital in the Boulevard. He also purchased the land for the
Winter Gardens and gifted it to the town by way of compensation for the damage
caused to the town's roads by his heavy quarry lorries. This was the closing chapter to
a long court case brought by the Council, and which Butt eventually lost, having
fought it all the way to the House of Lords. He died on 7 November 1944.

Henry Butt, Mayor of Weston Borough
Council, presenting prizes at a school
sports day, c.1938.

The Langford Rovers football team, 1938/39. There were several local teams around the town, often linked to a business or
locality such as the Gas Works or as in this case Langford Road. Matches were played at what was known as The Great
Ground, at the junction of Locking and Hutton Moor Roads.

Souvenir programme and newspaper advertisement for the opening
of the Odeon Cinema, Weston-super-Mare, 25 May 1935. This
building, designed by renowned architect Cecil Howitt, was state-of-
the-art for its time. As well as having air-conditioning, a newly-
patented acoustic material was used in the auditorium to assist
the hard-of-hearing. The opening ceremony was performed by
local MP, Ian Orr-Ewing, followed by the first recital on the
illuminated Compton Organ by Alfred Richards. This organ
was advertised as combining a full symphony orchestra, a modern
dance band and a cathedral organ. Every piece of the instrument
was manufactured in Britain and it is still in regular use today. The
first manager of the cinema was Mr W. Johns.

There were three other picture houses in the town in the 1930s – the
Tivoli in the Boulevard, the Central in Oxford St and the Regent in
Regent St. The Tivoli was lost in the blitz of June 1942. The
Central and Regent (later renamed the Gaumont) were both
demolished. Today there is only the Odeon, although plans have
been announced to include a 50-seat 4D cinema in the new Grand
Pier Pavilion.

After the opening film of *Brewsters' Millions,* forthcoming
attractions included *Wings in the Dark* with Cary Grant, *David
Copperfield* starring W.C. Fields and *After Office Hours* with Clark
Gable.

Autographed programme for a Sunday Concert by Reginald Foort on the Compton Organ at the Odeon Cinema, 15 January 1939. Foort was educated at the Royal College of Music and began his career playing accompaniments to silent movies. He began his recording career in 1932, and remains one of the most recorded organists in history. As well as performing all over the world, Foort was staff organist at the BBC and was featured regularly on either the BBC Concert Organ or its Theatre Organ. He left the BBC in 1951 and went to live in the USA. He died in Pasadena in 1980.

Weston-super-Mare Juniors Association Football Club, 1933/34.
They are pictured at the ground in Langford Road. The chimney in the background is that of the Royal Potteries. Four pencilled names on the reverse are Delafield, Powell and Davey. Mr R.W. Durnford is standing in the centre in the back row.

Weston-super-Mare Juniors Association Football Club, 1935/36.
Left to right, back row: ?, ?, ?, ?, ?, ?, Mr R.W. Durnford, Harry Lye; middle: ?, ?, R. Watt, ?, K. Lane; front: ?, ?.

Weston-super-Mare Juniors Association Football Club, 1935/36. Harry Lye (right) is giving the team a pep talk. Lye was later headmaster of The College and was a cousin of Sir Ralph Reader. Reader was born in Crewkerne in Somerset and was famed for starting the Scout Gang Shows in 1932.

Weston-super-Mare Juniors Association Football Club, 1936/37. That season they were winners of the Somerset County F. A. Intermediate Shield. Left to right, back row: Mr A. Wride, E. Price, Mr R.W. Durnford, H. Magor, F. Quick, C. Sperring, Mr A. Lane; centre: K. Windsor, R. Langdale (Vice Captain); front: W. Durston, R. Watt, K. Lane (Captain), A. Wride, V.J. Payne.

Their record that year was impressive with 26 games played of which they won 23, drew one and lost two. They scored 154 goals, with 28 goals scored against them.

Weston-super-Mare Juniors Association Football Club 1936/37 season.
Team Captain K. Lane being presented with the Somerset County Intermediate Football Trophy with the other team members lined up in front.

Weston-super-Mare Juniors Association Football Club after having won the Somerset County Intermediate Football Trophy, 1936/37 season.
Left to right: ?, ?, Mr Durnford, ?, ?, ?, R. Watt (holding shield), K. Lane, A. Wride, ?, ?, ?.

Treasurer and staff of Weston-super-Mare Urban District Council, 1930s.

St John's Ambulance volunteer nurses, c.1935.
Left to right, back row; ?, Elsie Phelps Tottle, Joyce Tidman; front: F. Langley, L. Lovill (L Division Superintendant), Lucy Bere (matron at Weston Hospital), H. Lowther; The photo was taken by R.W. Brown, High Street, Weston-super-Mare.

Mr Walter J. Tottle's Bakery shop at 17 Orchard Street, decorated for the Silver Jubilee of King George V, 1935. This shop was just opposite the junction with Cross Street. Today it is the Orient Fish Bar.

Jean Margaret Dashwood, aged 10, 1933. Jean was the daughter of local grocer William Dashwood who owned a shop in Meadow Street. She recalled that ,"When I was about seven years old I commenced at Miss Greta Cousins dancing school in Wilton Gardens. We wore short brown velvet dresses with slits at the sides. Every year she gave dancing displays at the Knightstone Pavilion. I enjoyed taking part in them but I had to leave off these classes when I began school at Eastern House." About 1941 Jean met Frank Cradock, brother of her best friend Phyllis, when he was home on leave from France. They married and had two children, Richard and Robert. Sadly Frank was killed in a road accident on 7 October 1955. Seven years later Jean met and later married local policeman Douglas Overy, mayor of Weston 1972/73.

Class from the Greta Cousins' dancing school, Wilton Gardens, June 1930. They are pictured just prior to a Dancing Display in aid of the Sunshine Homes for Blind Babies and the Sightless of Somerset. The performance was originally booked to be at the Grand Pier Pavilion, but because it had burnt down in January that year, the show was switched to the Knightstone Theatre. Over 50 youngsters took part in the three hour show. The entry pictured was on the theme of hunting, with a genuine huntsman and hounds!
Left to right, back row:?, ?, ?, ?, ?, Jean Dashwood, Betty Redding, Joan Redding. Standing in the middle at the front is Stuart Price.

Fuchsia Patrol of the Girl Guides, Burton House School, 1932. The school had its own Guide Company. One of the girls in the back row is Joyce Salisbury. The others are unknown.

Jean Palmer and Valerie Cutts, summer 1936. These Burton House School pupils are pictured returning to the school after a swimming lesson at Knightstone Baths.

Burton House School pupils and staff, July 1936. They are pictured in Ellenborough Park, which was close to the school on the corner of Walliscote and Albert Roads. Left to right, back row: Eileen Hammond, Joan Redding, Sylvia White, Betty Redding, June Stickland, Monica Burn, Mary Dant, Valerie Cutts, Dorothy Dennis, Pearl Smith, ?, Pam Thompson, Isis Millar, Nina Brooks, Valerie Gough, Joan Nancarrow, Pamela Armstrong, Pamela Smith, Margaret Evans; Third row: Eileen Hicks, Kay Payne, Maureen Champion, Mary Thompson, Dorothy Forrester, Mary Wood, Marjorie Legg, Mary Croker, ?, Mary Diment, ?, Jean Boyd, Sybil Rich, Barbara Fussell, ?, Mavis Dyson, ?, Margaret Betteridge, Connie Evans, Dawn Lee, Netta Weir, Ivy Cox; second row, l-r: Mary Moore, Freda Disney, Joan Rainey, Eileen Scott, Brenda Bonnett, Sybil Blake, Connie Williams, ?, Violet Hookins, Mary Russell, Jean Melvin (Brown Owl), Mrs Sumner, Miss C. Weir, Miss M. Agnew, Miss Edwards, Miss Callow, Mmselle de Coq, ?, June Kirkwood, ?, Margaret Pickett, Margaret Williams, Jean ?, Mary Price, Valerie Ashman; front: ?, Jacqueline Ellery, ?, Joy Clark, ?, Eileen Creed, ?, Ruth Louch, Anne Elliot, ?, ?, ?, ?, ?, ?, ?, ?, ?, ?, ?, ?, ?, ?, Janet Elliot, Olive Durbin, ? .

Drawing of the new Three Queens Hotel on the corner of Oxford Street and Union Street (now High Street South, and originally Gas Street) as it would look when completed for new proprietor, F. Denning. This modern building replaced a much older pub, still called the Three Queens. The image was published in the *Weston-super-Mare Gazette Pictorial*, 1933.

Members of the Weston Wheelers cycling club, c.1935. Left to right, back row: Mr Amesbury, ?, ?, Frances Meakin; front: Graham Cope, ?. The first Cycling Club in Weston was formed in 1878. By 1892, there were 109 members, meeting regularly at Huntley's Restaurant in Regent Street. In those days, the cyclists were preceded by a bugler as the cycles did not have bells. By 1933 the Club had reformed as the Weston Wheelers. The lady members kept the club going throughout the Second World War with the next official meet in 1946. They are still going, meeting regularly every Sunday for a Club Run. They are also one of the few clubs in North Somerset that hold a weekly summer evening time trial on a local course.

Part of a *Weston Gazette* supplement highlighting the changes to the town in the 1930s. Top left is the new Kewstoke Convalescent Home, opened in 1933. Top right is the building of Weston Grammar School, or the County School as it was then, opened in 1935. This was demolished in 1999 and Broadoak Community School built on the site. In the middle is the construction of shops in The Centre. Bottom left is the demolition of the Plough Hotel in High Street, next door to Burtons. Bottom right are some of the completed shops in The Centre. The 1930s were a period of huge investment in Weston, with many well-known buildings constructed during this decade, including the Open Air Pool, Odeon Cinema and Rozel Bandstand, as well as those in the picture.

Bonny Baby competition, 1933. These babies with their proud mothers are pictured at the summer fête held at Milton in aid of the funds for St Jude's Church. I wonder how many still live in the area today?

The Duke of Kent chats to some people with disabilities while on a visit to Weston-super-Mare, 27 June 1935. He was in the town to officially name the new lifeboat. This was Weston's first motor lifeboat and replaced the sail and oar-driven *Colonel Stock*. The new boat was funded out of a legacy left to the RNLI by the late C. Ashley and the name was derived from the first names of Mr Ashley and his wife – Fifi and Charles. Built in the Isle of Wight, the *Fifi & Charles* was sent to Weston in 1933 and was first launched on service the following year when the supply boat for Steep Holm lost power in choppy seas and strong winds. The naming ceremony for the *Fifi & Charles* took place at Knightstone in front of a crowd of thousands. The day began with the royal party attending a lunch at the Royal Pier Hotel as the guests of Mr Jackson-Barstow. On his way to Knightstone the Duke reviewed a guard of honour formed by local members of the Royal British Legion before performing the naming ceremony by breaking a bottle of Somerset cider over the lifeboat's bow. Over her 29 years of service the *Fifi & Charles* was launched 68 times, and saved 83 lives. Prince George, Duke of Kent and fourth son of King George V and Queen Mary, was the President of the RNLI. In the photograph, the lady in the dark coat, leaning over the railing, is Margery Gooding.

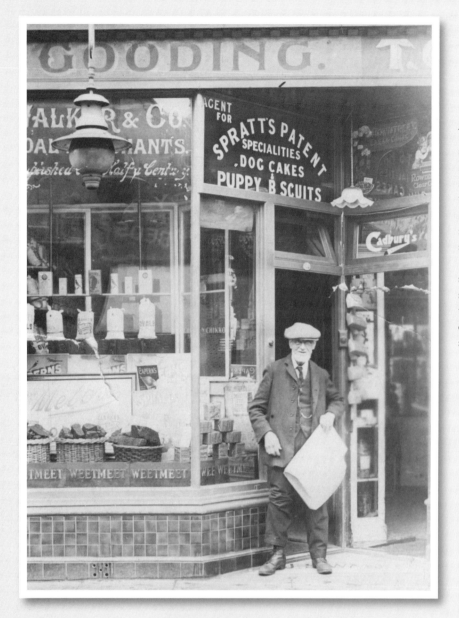

William Henry Gooding outside his shop in Regent Place, Weston, c.1932. Regent Place was a little lane off Regent Street, roughly opposite where the Silica stands today. Vowles' Livery Stables and mews used to be there, along with the Waggon & Horses Pub and a number of cottages. By the 1930s, there was just Mr Gooding's shop and the Weston Motor Co. Ltd., along with a few cottages. It was one of the areas demolished in the huge town centre rebuilding scheme of the 1950s and 1960s.

Dorothy Gooding with her brother Gordon, pictured at Madeira Cove in the early 1930s.

Dorothy Gooding and Ernest "Yorkie" Mattison in the back yard of Dorothy's home in Regent Place, Weston-super-Mare, July 1939. Dorothy was the daughter of William Gooding who ran a coal merchant business. Dorothy and Ernest later married (see page 46).

FUSSELL'S SPORTS CLUB CRICKET TEAM

If
it is
made
of
Rubber

Please
send
us
your
Enquiry

FUSSELL'S RUBBER Co., Ltd.
WORLE
The Manufacturers of "RUBROX" RUBBER SOLES, HEELS, MATS, Etc.

Picture of the Fussell's Rubber Co. cricket team, originally published in the *Weston Gazette Pictorial*, 1933. The factory was at 11 Station Road, Worle. When the factory was moved to St Georges, the Worle site was bought by McCarthy & Stone Ltd, to develop with 46 sheltered flats and ten affordable housing flats.

Annie Elizabeth Bryan (right). On the left is her sister Mary, who was married to one of the Radmilovic family. Paulo Radmilovic was famous as an Olympic Gold Medallist swimmer, winning four gold medals in three successive games. He was also a member of the local water polo team. Although born in Wales, he lived in Weston for many years before his death here in 1968. Mary later divorced and in 1923 married Sam Gummer, following which they emigrated to Canada.
The sisters are pictured with Annie's dog, Smudge at her home, Highfield, Worlebury, c.1938.

Local Auctioneer and Estate Agent, George "Bunt" Bryan at Knightstone, c.1935.

Advertisement for the Li-Lo air bed, available at John Moore's sports shop in High Street North, 1935. The 1930s were the decade when sun-bathing and swimming became really popular. The new open air pool in Weston was even built with sun-bathing platforms. Previously a sun tan was seen as the mark of someone who worked outdoors, probably as a labourer or field worker and therefore lower class. When the majority of people began to work in factories and offices, a sun tan proved you either had plenty of leisure time to spend outdoors, or could afford a foreign holiday. The "lifeboat" reference is because the advert appeared in the edition reporting on the naming of Weston's new lifeboat, *Fifi & Charles*.

The 1940s

The long years of the Second World War brought many changes to Weston. Some were obvious, such as the destruction caused by bombing raids, which destroyed many parts of the town centre. Some were more intangible, like the social changes brought about by the departure of men, to the battlefronts, the arrival of evacuees and refugees and the opening up of new job opportunities to women.

Weston was not a safe haven from bombs, as had been hoped when people in cities such as Birmingham, Bristol and the East End of London evacuated their children here. Two major blitzes took place in 1941 and 1942, killing and injuring hundreds. Additionally there were several smaller attacks, particularly when planes jettisoned bombs intended for the docks and industrial areas of Cardiff and Bristol. Around 150 people died and over 500 were injured in Weston alone between 1940 and 1945. Many hotels and guest houses were requisitioned for use as Red Cross hospitals or billets for newly drafted soldiers who were posted to the town for training. In 1944 Weston played host to hundreds of US troops in the build up to the Normandy Landings. Despite all this, some people still managed to come here on holiday and in the summer months the papers were full of morale-boosting images of happy mothers and children on the beach.

Morale was also kept up by the formation of new clubs and groups. Friendships were made that lasted well beyond the War, and around 150 evacuee families decided to make Weston their permanent home. Despite the struggles of these years, people still look back on them with a fondness, probably for the community spirit they fostered.

Westonians were quick to offer their services to a whole raft of volunteer organisations, from the Red Cross Voluntary Aid Detachment nurses or the Women's Royal Voluntary Service, to the Home Guard and Air Raid Wardens. Those men serving in the Auxiliary Fire Service even travelled to help in the blitzes on Bristol and Exeter, a deed reciprocated in Weston's hour of need.

On the positive side, the War brought new industries to the town, chiefly aircraft production. Avro Anson training aircraft were built at the Western Airways site and Bristol Beaufighters at Oldmixon. Many of these factories remained after peace was declared, swapping their products from military to civilian needs such as pre-fabricated buildings to ease the housing shortages.

Whilst rationing lasted well into the following decade, the last years of the 1940s were full of optimism and hope that a new town would rise phoenix-like from the ashes of war. It would not do so without some accompanying birthing pains however.

Bomb damage in Waterloo Street, 1942. The nights of 28 and 29 June that year saw the biggest air raids on Weston yet. Around 97 bombs and 10,000 incendiaries fell on the town over the two nights, causing the death of over 100 people, together with widespread destruction of property. Another 400 people were injured and 3,000 made homeless by the raids. Waterloo Street and the Boulevard were one area hit, with the loss of Lance & Lance's department store, the Boulevard Congregational Church and the Tivoli Cinema. The middle part of South Parade and the Wadham Street Baptist Church were all set alight. The men of the Auxiliary Fire Service did a sterling job, assisted by fire crews from as far afield as Exeter. Water was pumped from Marine Lake and static water tanks that were situated throughout the town, including one in Alexandra Parade. It was not only bombs that presented a danger. Some of the enemy aircraft flew low along some streets, including the Boulevard, machine-gunning anyone unlucky enough to be out in the open. Today, some of the bombed areas can still be identified by the modern buildings amongst the older ones. Look at the corner of Orchard Street opposite Burlington Street and there is a row of 1950s shops, built just after the War. On the corner of High Street and Waterloo Street, Argos and its adjacent shops are noticeably different from those further down each road.

La Retraite First X1 Hockey Team, 1948/49.

La Retraite was a Roman Catholic private girls' school in South Road, Weston. It was founded in 1898 when Canon Barron, priest at St Joseph's Church in Camp Road, wrote to the Mother Superior of the convent of La Retraite at Burnham on Sea asking the Sisters to come to Weston and open an elementary school and day school in the town. Five Sisters arrived the following year and set up in a rented house in Paragon Road. At that time Roman Catholics were often regarded with suspicion and the Sisters were no exception, especially as four of them were French, and the early years were not easy. A small day school was opened in Florence Villa, Quarry Road, but the Sisters struggled to find pupils. At the same time they were looking for a larger house to open as a boarding school. In 1904 there were no day pupils left and just three lady-boarders at the Paragon Road house. A new Mother Superior, Reverend Mother St Pacome, helped to make ends meet by giving private lessons in French and painting and gradually the local people began to lose their suspicions of them. Three years later 30 pupils were being taught in the elementary school, now situated in Fortfield in South Road next door to a boys' school run by Mr Ibbs. When Mr Ibbs left in 1910, the Sisters were able to acquire the property and open a secondary school for girls. This became La Retraite. When the Second World War broke out the pupils were evacuated to Brinsop Court in Herefordshire and the South Road building was leased to the Red Cross as a hospital for war-wounded soldiers. The Red Cross stayed in the building until 19 May 1946 and much work was needed before the school returned from Hereford. In the 1960s La Retraite saw further expansion in numbers as well as in academic achievement, as an increasing number of pupils went on to university. Unfortunately it was not to last. In common with many private schools at the time, La Retraite was forced to close the Weston school in 1971, amalgamating with La Retraite at Burnham on Sea.

Sixth form pupils at
La Retraite School, 1949.

Sewing staff at Moorland Laundry, Moorland Road, Weston, 1939-45. Many of the hotels and guest houses as well as larger private homes used Moorland Road Laundry. Repair and mending services were even more important during the Second World War, when "Make Do and Mend" became the order of the day.

Bridge Road VE Day party, May 1945. All over the country, Victory tea parties were held in the streets in the weeks following the end of the Second World War in Europe on 8 May 1945. For the first time in six years, street lights were allowed back on, neighbours pooled ration coupons to create a good spread of food and pianos were wheeled out to provide music for dancing in the streets. In Weston the first street to hold a party was Osborne Road, on Tuesday 16 May. Many others followed including Wellsea and Moorland Roads, Lonsdale Avenue, George Street and Stradling Avenue. The latter held their party in "Bomb Alley" as it was nicknamed after a 1000lb bomb fell there in the raids of 1942. In the celebrations in Holland Street they roasted an effigy of Hitler.

More parties were held in August to celebrate Victory over Japan and the final end of the Second World War. Some of the communities that staged parties on this occasion were Chesham, Sandford and Parkhurst Roads, Union, Wadham and Alma Streets and Milton Brow.

Another VE Day party photograph. This one is in the playground of Worle Infant School, May 1945, when residents of The Rows, Spring Hill and Coronation Road all got together to throw one big party to celebrate the end of the Second World War. In recent years, John Durston, who had attended the Hill Road East VJ (Victory in Japan) Day party, and had a treasured photograph of everyone who was there, was inspired to organise a reunion just over 60 years later. Dozens of people who had been at the original street party met up again in Hill Road East at 11am on 16 August, 2006.

More VE Day celebrations, this time in Furland Road, Milton, May 1945. Among those in the picture are David and Gertrude Clark, their daughter-in-law Mrs Clark and her two children (one with the drum), Ernest and Rosina Milkins, May Tottle with her children Peter and Ann, Vera Taylor, William and Marjorie Blewitt and their son John, Mrs Smith with her son John, Mrs James, George Banger and his wife and son Paul, Mrs Pike, Mrs Cox, Sydney Redman, John Hayden, Cornelius Fear, Mrs Hadley, John Stabbins, Beatrice Hoddinott with her five sons, Dora College and Terry Hadley. Mrs Hoddinott worked at the Thatched Cottage Restaurant in Knightstone Road, which loaned teapots for the celebration.

Another view of the street party in Furland Road, Milton, May 1945. The newspaper reported that the events were interrupted by rainstorms – you can see the wet road in this photo! Some of these children were quite likely to be evacuees. Of the hundreds of women and children evacuated to Weston from cities such as Birmingham and Bristol and the East End of London, 149 families stayed in the town after the War making it their permanent home.

Another picture of the Furland Road VE Day celebrations, Milton, May 1945. This time just the adults are featured.
Left to right, back row: Mrs Fisher, Mrs James, Mrs Hayden, Mrs Nicholas, Amy Colburn, Eddy Colburn;
Middle row: Mrs Ruby Gollege, Mrs Banger, ?, ?, Mr Banger, unknown soldier behind, ?, Mrs Kerslake, ?, Edna ?, ?, ?, Mr Crocket, Mrs D. Clark, Mr James, ?, Mr Ernest Milkins, Mr Hoddinot, Mrs Hoddinot, Mr Redman, ?, Mrs Redman, Mrs Fear, ?, ?, ?, Mrs Cox, ?, ?, ?, Mrs R. Clark, Mr Cornelius Fear; Front row: Rose Colburn, Margery Blewitt, Mrs May Tottle, ?, Mrs Pike, ? (with baby), Mrs Crocket, Mr Fisher, Mrs Hadley, ? (with baby), Mrs Knight.

Co-owners and the manager of the Grand Pier, standing in front of the Pavilion, c.1949. Left to right: George Davey (Pier Manager), ?, Derek Brenner (co-owner and son of George Brenner), ?, George Brenner (co-owner), Arnold Brenner (co-owner and son of George Brenner), Mr Palmer (Company Secretary).

At this period the pier was open late into the evenings, with a ballroom and restaurant as well as amusements. Dancing and supper cost 5/6d (27½p) per person in 1939. It was normal for people to change into evening dress for dinner when dining out and so the Brenners decided that the staff should change into dinner jackets as well.

The Grand Pier "White Coat crew", c.1949. They are pictured near the entrance to the pier, where the wooden decking changes to tarmac. Left to right: ? (Assistant Toll Master), Fred Frost (Tollmaster), George Brenner (co-owner), ?, ?, ?

The Boulevard, c.1940. The cars in the middle of the road are parked there. At the time there was a central lane down the centre of the road, marked out for parking, not that there would be many cars in use in the war years due to strict petrol rationing. On the right is the entrance to the Tivoli Cinema. This suffered a direct hit in the bombing raids of 28/29 June 1942.

Weston Youth Cricket Team versus Stourbridge match, played at the Recreation Ground on Wednesday 24 August 1949. Stourbridge beat Weston by one wicket. K. Jacobs and B. Fry opened for Weston, with Fry being the top scorer with 31. Team Captain Rodney Berkeley hit 17. Other players were E. Barrett, G. Marsh, Mr Harrison, Mr Boaler, Mr Thorne and T. Osborne.

Mr and Mrs Baker, 80 George Street, Weston-super-Mare, c.1949. This photograph was lent by Ernie Hooper. Mr Hooper grew up on a farm in Wedmore with his parents, seven brothers and two sisters. At the age of 15, and unable to find work in the village, he came to Weston where he got a job with Mrs Payne at her bakery in Whitecross Road. He lodged with Charlie and Mrs Baker at their house at 80 George Street for a weekly rent of £1.10s (£1.50). His weekly earnings were just £1.15s (£1.75), so very often Mrs Baker gave him some money back so he was able to go to the cinema or out in town. The Bakers' had lost their only son Charles, who was a sailor on HMS *Hood*, when it was sunk by the German battleship *Bismarck* in May 1941. On receiving the news the shock had made Mrs Baker go deaf and Ernie remembers having to shout very loudly for her to hear. When her favourite comic song, "With her Head Tucked Underneath her Arm", performed by Stanley Holloway, came on the radio it would be turned up to full volume and she would put her ear to the speaker and stay there laughing.

Charlie Baker had fought in the trenches in the First World War. In his waistcoat pocket he carried a penny with a dent in the middle. This had saved his life when he was hit by a bullet which the coin deflected. He worked in Chards, an off licence and grocer's on the corner of Baker Street and Swiss Road, and was a keen follower of the town rugby team and also played billiards.

The Duke of Kent talks to volunteers after the blitz, 10 July 1942. The dreadful blitzes on Weston on the nights of the 28 and 30 June, 1942, left the town in a state of devastation and shock. The town was full of holidaymakers, many of them munitions workers on a much-needed break. Over the two nights around 97 high explosive bombs and over 10,000 incendiaries were dropped. By the Sunday night the whole of Weston looked to be ablaze. As the people began to pick themselves up, news came that the Duke of Kent wanted to pay a personal tribute to the people and volunteers for the way they had coped. Many of those working in First Aid, Rescue and Casualty Clearing worked the whole 48 hours non-stop. After a tour of the worst areas, including the Bournville Estate and Orchard Street, where the loss of life had been heaviest the Duke commented to the Mayor, Alderman R. Hosken, 'Your people are magnificent.' He then met some of the hundreds of volunteers as they paraded on the Beach Lawns, in front of some of the homes wrecked by the raids. Elsie Phelps Tottle is in the dark uniform immediately to his left. The small lady to the right of the Ambulance Service sign is Edith Chapman.

The Duke of Kent was killed the following month when the flying boat in which he was a passenger crashed into a hillside near Caithness in bad weather.

Elsie Phelps Tottle in her St John's Ambulance Brigade nurses uniform. She is pictured with the Henry Butt Challenge Cup for "Public Utilities & Transport" which she won for working 981 hours as a First Aid Patrol volunteer between 1 January and 31 December, 1940.

Elsie Phelps Tottle with her dog Mick, pictured at her home at 1 Whitting Road, Weston, c.1941. She is dressed in her working uniform as a First Aid Patrol nurse. First Aid Parties were formed mostly from volunteers from the St John Ambulance Brigade (as in Elsie's case) or the Red Cross. There were eight parties of four manning the two Weston Depots, plus drivers and messengers, with three more parties at Worle.

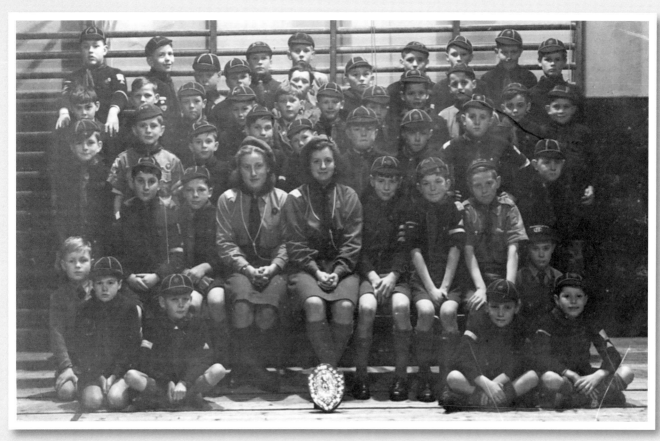

First YMCA Cubs, pictured in the YMCA Gymnasium in the High Street, Weston, c.1948. The fair boy without a cap on the left is Jeffrey Archer, later to become a politician and best-selling author. The Archer family only moved to Weston from Mark in 1944. Derek Tottle is seated immediately to the right of the Cub Mistress.

First YMCA Cubs, pictured at their camp at Congresbury, c.1948. Left to right, back row: Peter Slade, ?, Jeff Hynds (Rover Scout and helper) David Thorpe, Babs Baker, Bill Holly, Mrs Holly (Akela); middle row: ?, ?, ?, Robert Lovell, Maurice Braithewaite; front: ?, Phillip Sutton, Derek Tottle, ?, ?, Jeffrey Archer, Nicky Dunstone, ?, ?.

First YMCA Scouts parade down the High Street, Weston, c.1948.

John and Edith Chapman pictured on VE Day, 5 May 1945 in the garden of their home at Swiss Road, Weston. Edith was a member of the Tottle family, who ran a bakery business in Orchard Street, Weston. They are both wearing uniforms of the St John's Ambulance Brigade and both served as volunteers in First Aid Parties throughout the Second World War. Edith's sister Elsie was also a St John's nurse.

Victoria Bowling Club, Albert Quadrant, Weston, 1946. This is the oldest of Weston's three outdoor bowling clubs, opening in April 1900. The others are at Ashcombe and Clarence Parks. The club has the distinction of having provided no less than three presidents of the English Bowling Association. The captain, William Dashwood, is seated on the lawn on the left at the very front.

The Ship Inn Outing, 1947. These were annual events organised by the pub's regulars.
Left to right, back row: Derek Clark (on bus), Mrs Clark, Mr Wilshaw, Jacky Porter, ?, ?, ?, Jack Hancock, H. Bowden;
Third row: Sam Counsell (driver), H. Williams, Mr Staples, H. Raymond, ?, ?, Arthur Huxtable, F. Scott, H. Shepherd, David Minifie, ?, Mrs Williams, ?, Mrs Counsell, ?, ?; Second row: Fred Bream, Doris Bream, ?, Tom Tucker, ?, Bertha Tucker, Jean Huxtable, Mrs Stevenson, Minnie Pople, Doreen Counsell, Beryl Middle, Mrs Scott, ?, Lil Price, Bert Long; front row (seated): Mrs Shepherd, Gillian Raymond, Mrs Raymond, Mrs Ellard, Elsie Huxtable, Win Ellard, Ethel Long, Mrs Middle, Annie King, Mrs Porter, Bert Middle (driver).

Phyllis Cradock and Jean Dashwood pictured in Burlington Street, Weston in their Red Cross Voluntary Aid Detachment uniforms, 1940. In 1938, and with the country under threat of war, Jean joined the Red Cross Somerset 16 Detachment under commandant, Mrs Tucker. She studied first aid and home nursing and it was there she met Phyllis, who was five years older. When war broke out, several Weston properties were commandeered as Red Cross hospitals, including Highcroft in Eastfield Park, the large house on the corner of Ashcombe and Clarendon Road and the Grand Central Hotel. The girls also worked at the General Hospital, the Sanatorium on Beach Road and at the camp hospital at RAF Locking.

Red Cross Voluntary Aid nurses from Somerset 16 Detachment, on the roof of the Grand Central Hotel in Weston-super-Mare, 1940. The hotel was one of several properties requisitioned as Red Cross Hospitals for the duration of the war. Left to right, back row: Mrs Perkins, Miss Wickendon, Mary Wall, ?; front row: ?, ?, Jean Dashwood, Miss Hare.

Red Cross nurses of the Voluntary Aid Detachments at the Salute to Soldiers Parade, Weston, April 1944. The third nurse down on the right is Mollie Bryan. The Voluntary Aid Detachment (VAD) was an organisation, founded by the British Red Cross and the Order of St John of Jerusalem in 1909, to provide auxiliary nursing services to hospitals in time of war. Other VAD volunteers also became fundraisers, cooks, kitchen maids, clerks, ward-maids, letter writers for patients and ambulance drivers. They played a vital role in keeping hospitals running, caring for the sick and running First Aid Posts, under often difficult conditions. In the June 1942 air raid, three nurses were injured when a bomb fell close to the First Aid Post at the Open Air Pool. In addition to fixed posts throughout Weston, there was also a mobile unit available, consisting of a caravan fitted up as a mobile operating theatre, and a car to carry a doctor, nurse, and a team of Red Cross and St John Ambulance personnel.

Freda Crichton in the garden of her home at 29, Southville Road, Weston, c.1944.

The wartime wedding of Jean Dashwood and Frank Cradock, Boulevard Methodist Church, 15 July 1943. It was Phyllis who introduced her brother Frank to Jean when she asked her if she would write to him as a pen friend while he was stationed in France. It was the beginning of the Second World War and Frank was serving in the RAF. They met when he came home on leave after being evacuated from Dunkirk, and continued to correspond with each other. They got engaged in 1943 but were not considering marrying until Frank got a posting abroad again. He managed to get a special licence and the wedding took place on his embarkation leave. After the wedding they all went back to Jean's home at 51 The Boulevard for a small reception. For their honeymoon they had a few days at the Piper's Inn at Ashcott, before a policeman called to say Frank's leave was cancelled and he had to report to West Kirby in the Wirral. When he arrived there he found his orders had been changed and he was given a few more days back home with his new wife before being posted to Kenya, where he was stationed for the next two and a half years.

Left to right, back row: Dorothy Payne, Mr Griffiths, Mr Dashwood (father of the bride), Phyllis Jenkins (née Cradock and sister of the groom), Joan Davies, Frank Cradock, Ada Crichton, Jean Dashwood, Nancy Muir, Mrs Griffiths, Freda Crichton, F. Cradock, ?; front row: Alice Hogg (maternal grandmother of the bride), Dorothy Cradock, Fanny Sykes, Greta Dashwood. Dorothy Payne was the daughter of Bill Payne who was the licensee of the Elm Tree Inn in Meadow Street. Joan Davies' father farmed at Ebdon Farm, Worle.

Air raid warden with siren. The first bombs fell on
Weston in August 1940, exploding on the beach.
From then on there were regular incidents,
including two major blitzes in January 1941 and
June 1942. There were few communal shelters as in
the cities, and most people on hearing the siren
would use their personal shelters. These came in
two types – the Anderson, which was a corrugated
iron construction designed to be part buried in the
garden, or the Morrison, which was like a large
heavy table with wired sides and you sheltered
underneath it. Some people just went down into
their cellars or under the stairs.

This photograph was reputedly taken on the roof of
the Gaslight Company Workshops and Stores in
Burlington Street, Weston, c.1940. This building
was converted into the award-winning North
Somerset Museum in 1974. However, at the time of writing, plans have been announced to sell it together with the
adjoining cottages and old chapel, and move the museum collections to an as yet unnamed site.

Embroidered tablecloth worked by H.R.
Hendey, 1939. The cloth commemorates
events of the Second World War, both
national and local. The Hendey family
lived in Bristol, moving to Weston in
October 1944. Various events are
embroidered all around the edges. The
centre part of the cloth bears the names of
70 family and friends, signed in pen or
pencil and embroidered over. Some of the
names are struck through in black with the
date of their death embroidered next to
them. It is a moving memorial to one
family's experience of war. The names
listed include H.L. & E.M. Reed, C.H.
Barrington, Edward Hendey, M. Higgison,
W. Hendey (died 8 Jan 1941), S.K. Hendey,
Fred and Doris Cottrell, H.G. Hendey,
E. & A.J. Gillingham, L. Painter, M. J.
Ham, E. Pottinger, E. Cavanagh, S. Hendey
(died 22 January 1943), S. Webber, E Stagg,
E. Christopher (died 20 March 1943),
A. Priddle, Pat Bryant, P. S. Plummer,
L. Haskins, Vera Mitchell and E.V. Dunn.
The current owner of this cloth, David
Kidd, bought it at an antique fair and
would welcome any further information on
its history.

Two pictures of Gordon Gooding of Weston-super-Mare. The portrait photo shows Sapper Gordon Gooding of the Welsh Guards, 1943. The full-length photo was taken in Ashcombe Park in May 1946. Gordon was the son of William Henry Gooding, Coal Merchant of Regent Place, Weston. Gordon was so keen to "do his bit" for the war effort he lied about his age so he could join the Home Guard in 1941, when he was just 16 years old. As soon as he turned 18, he joined up, serving in the 1st Battalion, Welsh Guards, attached to the Guards Armoured Division and was among the first troops to enter Brussels. After the War he returned to Weston and helped his father in the family Coal Merchant's business in Regent Place.

William Gooding, coal merchant of Regent Place, Weston, with his daughter Dorothy at her wedding to Ernest Mattison.

The wartime wedding of Ernest Mattison and Dorothy Gooding. Left to right, back row: Elizabeth Gooding, ?, William Henry Gooding, ?, ?, ?; front row: Margery Gooding with John Gooding in front of her, Dorothy Gooding, Ernest Matttison, ?.

Muriel Bryan with her children Jennifer and John, pictured at Knightstone, 1944.

Mollie Bryan with her dog, Rufus at her new home at 39 Charlton Road, Weston, c.1948.

Mollie Bryan with her dog Smudge at her home at Highfield, Worlebury Hill, 1940.

The Salvation Army Songsters, 1949. They are lined up ready to march off singing with the band following, probably for an open air service on the beach. They always used the area of the sands between the Grand Pier and the public toilets. Beatrice Bressington often preached, attracting large crowds who lined the wall and the side of the Pier to listen. Mrs Bressington and her husband were also caretakers of the Salvation Army Citadel in Carlton Street.

Army Cadets at the Langford Road Drill Hall, Weston-super-Mare, 1943.

The 1950s

The decade from 1950 to 1959 saw the country emerge from a make-do-and-mend attitude to one of mass consumerism. The war had exposed people to new ideas and values. Youth culture was developing (the word "teenager" was first used in the early 1950s) and coffee bars and clubs were opened to cater for them. Unemployment was low and increasing disposable income made it acceptable for young people to care about what they looked like and to dress for show instead of just having work or school clothes and Sunday-best. The Festival of Britain in 1951 and the coronation of the young Queen Elizabeth II in 1953 were good opportunities for the town to celebrate and relax after the long years of austerity.

Weston-super-Mare had to consider its future. While the traditional week at the seaside was still the normal holiday for most families, new developments in air travel and the accessibility of foreign resorts would soon impact on this. The streets, and indeed people, were still scarred by the war years and the Borough Council had to plan how to rebuild Weston. Rather than replace what was lost, they took the radical step of looking at further demolition and building a brand new town centre, to the extent of re-routing roads such as the Boulevard and Waterloo Street. The proposal that met with fierce controversy and anger however was the proposed demolition of more than 100 homes in the Carlton Street area. Most of the residents were aged between 52 and 89 and, in most cases, had lived there all their lives. A public enquiry was held and a year later the Minister of Housing gave a temporary reprieve to 50 properties. The remainder were marked down for demolition. Due to funding issues the full scheme never went ahead however and in the end there was piecemeal redevelopment and replacement of bombed buildings.

The war had brought much-needed work opportunities to Weston, among them aircraft production. In 1958 the Borough Council decided to actively promote Weston as a base for light industry, playing on its long association with the Midlands to encourage some firms to move to Weston by offering to sell or lease sites or buildings along Winterstoke Road. Council housing was also made available for those workers wishing to move here.

Despite the legacy of the Second World War, residents and tourists had plenty of facilities available to them throughout this period. There were three cinemas and four theatres offering a wide range of entertainment. In addition there were band concerts at Grove Park and the Rozel in summer. You could swim in the Open Air Pool and Knightstone swimming baths or undergo a therapeutic treatment at Knightstone Medicinal Baths. Weston Airport reopened after the War offering a reduced service of daily flights to Cardiff, summer pleasure flights and air taxis to any part of Britain. Steamers sailed from Birnbeck Pier throughout the summer and local news was covered by two weekly newspapers.

The Mayor's Christmas Fund, 23 December, 1958. Gifts were donated by members of the public for distribution to underprivileged children and the elderly and others in impoverished circumstances. The mayor Cllr L. Holtby is seen here with the manager of the Odeon Cinema, Mr Bigwood, who allowed the cinema to be used as a collection point.

Dining room of the Welbeck Hotel, 1950s. This hotel, on the corner of Knightstone Road and Greenfield Place, is still in business today, currently offering 23 en-suite rooms. It is now run by Mr and Mrs Phelps.

Waterloo Street, 1 November 1958. The bomb site was caused in 1942 when Lance & Lance department store took a direct hit. The site was temporarily used as a car park until new shops were built there in 1960. Interestingly, all the traffic seems to be facing east, although I am not aware Waterloo Street was ever a one-way street.

Clarks' shoe factory, 1958. This was in Whitecross Road. When Clarks built a new factory off Locking Road, this building was bought by Peggy Nisbet as a costume-doll-making factory. When she in turn moved production to a new building in Oldmixon Crescent, this became a Dance Studio. It has now been demolished and the site used for housing.

Tom Davis, using a skim net on Weston Beach in the 1950s. Skim nets were just one of the specialised methods used for fishing in the shallow waters of Weston and Bridgwater Bays. It took a lot of strength and skill to operate these heavy and unwieldy tools. The net was lowered and pushed forward through the water, and then lifted out with hopefully some fish trapped inside. One surviving example can (at the time of writing) be seen on display in North Somerset Museum in Burlington Street, Weston.

Summer Carnival float, advertising the opening of the Garden of Fragrance, Grove Park, 24 July 1958. The Garden of Fragrance was specifically designed for the sight impaired, with scented flowers, hand rails and Braille labels.

Uphill Castle Cricket Club, winners of the Weston-super-Mare and Axbridge District Youth Cricket Championship, 1950 season.
Left to right, back row: B. Bush, B.L. Browning, J. Wormleighton, J.R. Atkin, R.M. Bees, D.H. Prosser, B. Lewis, P. Taylor; front row: G. Stocker, B.J. Scott, R.V. Berkeley, B.E. Fry (Captain), D.W. Price, M.J. Farr, A.J. Trott.

A framed copy of this photograph was presented to R.W. Durnford by the Uphill Castle Cricket Club as a token of appreciation of all the work he had put into the youth teams.

Ashbrooke House School, summer 1955.
Ashbrooke House School in Ellenborough Park North, was founded by Kenneth and Margaret Thompson in September 1953 as an independent preparatory school for boys from ages 7 to 13. In 1963 the Thompsons sold the school to Lawrence and Joy Pickford who made the decision to admit girls. In 1989 David Atkinson bought the school. He shared the headship with Andrew Counsell and modernised it, adding a reception class and upgrading the facilities. It is now run by John and Angela Teasdale and has over 100 pupils.

Ashbrooke House School, summer 1956.

Trevor Schofield's Ballroom Dance Classes 16 March 1953. Trevor Schofield was a maths teacher at St John's School in Lower Church Road, starting there in 1946 after being demobbed from the RAF. He first started teaching dancing in St Jude's Hall at Milton in 1947. He continued to teach in various church halls and hotel ballrooms, until 1957 when he moved to a permanent studio in North Street, in what was originally the function room of Browns Café. Trevor and his wife Pat were pioneers in formation dancing and the Trevor Schofield Formation Team appeared on the BBC's Come Dancing shows for ten years. He retired in 1980 and died five years later at just 69 years of age.

Broadoak Rangers football team, Weston-super-Mare, season 1950/51. Unfortunately I have not been able to find out anything about this team, but some readers may recognise the faces?

Weston-super-Mare & District Lewin Youth Cup team at the match final at Wells, season 1957/58. The Lewin Cup is owned by the Somerset County Football Association and is a perpetual trophy competed for annually by teams who are affiliated to the Association.

Weston-super-Mare & District Association Football League Youth XI, season 1956/57. They are pictured at Wells on 29 April 1957, where they beat Midsummer Norton by 3 goals to 0. Left to right, back row: M.Rowley, T. Willets, ?, A Ricketts, ?, T. Black (goalkeeper), J. Fairhurst (full-back), R. Cole (centre forward); front row: D.A.Ward, K. Miles, A. Bass (captain), C. King, N. Barrett.

Weston-super-Mare Gas Company Sports Club "Knuts" Skittles Team, 1955. The photograph includes Ken Matthews and Mr Bucknell but unfortunately the other people are un-named. It was taken by F. Hardwick who owned a studio in Oxford Street, Weston.

Cooks and kitchen staff at the school kitchens on the Bournville Estate, early 1950s.

The school kitchens, early 1950s. This central facility turned out hundreds of school meals every day. The big vats were used to make custard!

St John's Secondary Modern School, Lower Church Road, Weston, late 1950s. This school closed on 24 July 1964 and was demolished two years later. Weston Technical College, as it was then, was built on the site. Among the children in this photograph are Peter Nichols, Stuart Hibbert, Alan Merrick, David Jones, Linda Mold, Carol Davies and Rickson Hough.

Walliscote Infant School end-of-year concert, July 1955.
Left to right, back row: ?, ?, ?, ?, ?, ?, ?, ?, ?; third row: ?, ?, ?, ?, ?, Adrian Clarke, ?, ?, ?, ?, ?, ?; second row: Peter Stradling, ?, ?, Michael Board, ?, ?, ?, ?, ?, ?; front: David Irving, ?, Alan Merrick, ?, ?, ?, Jill ?, ?, David Tanner.

Walliscote Infant School, Weston-super-Mare, 1957. The teacher is Mrs Ward. In the front row, from the left are: ?, Alan Merrick, Keith Craddock, Alan ?, ?, ?, ?, ?. On the right, between the girl and boy in the front is David Jones.

Walliscote Junior School, 4 July 1957. A special pageant was presented by three hundred pupils as part of the school's Diamond Jubilee celebrations. Excerpts from "Tom Brown's Schooldays", "Nicholas Nickleby" and "Billy Bunter" formed part of the all-day event with the theme "The Struggle for Learning". The performance was in the school playground in front of parents, friends and invited guests, including Alderman Mrs Eve Miller-Barstow, chairman of the County Education Committee. The pageant was devised by headmaster Mr P. Bunney and showed children's learning through the ages, from the earliest monastic schools, then the nineteenth century Dames' Schools to the opening of Walliscote School in 1897 and even an impression of a school in the future – with children in the inevitable space helmets! The pageant was interspersed with songs by the school choir and dancing by pupils, taught by Miss James of the Mavdor School of Dance. The photograph shows the scene from "Tom Brown's Schooldays".

Walliscote Junior School end-of-term display for parents, June 1954.

Burton House School. This private school for girls was founded in 1886 by Frances Maxwell Weir. Mrs Weir was the widow of a school inspector and came from Youghal in County Cork, Ireland with her seven children. Once in Weston, she established Burton House School, firstly at 15 Ellenborough Crescent, before moving to 6 Wilton Gardens and lastly, in around 1913, to a property on the north east corner of Walliscote Road and Albert Road. The Wilton Gardens property became Winthorpe School, run by Greta Cousins. As numbers grew at Burton House, the kindergarten was moved to a property at 32 Clevedon Road. Day girls were taken from the ages of five to sixteen, and there was a preparatory day school for boys aged five to eight. Mrs Weir remained principal until her death in 1932, when her daughters took over. In 1930 two classrooms were added, together with five bedrooms so boarding girls could be accommodated. By the end of the Second World War a staff of 12 (six resident and six visiting) taught 165 children. Perhaps the school's most distinguished ex-pupil was astronomer Sir Arthur Eddington, whose sister was later a teacher at the school. The school had its own Guide Company and during World War Two formed a Junior Red Cross Unit. By 1961 numbers had fallen to just 80 children and this, together with the death of Charlotte Weir, one of the two joint Principals, led to the decision to close the school.

Burton House School, May 1955. This picture of pupils and staff was taken in Ellenborough Park.
Left to right, back row: Pamela Cole, ?, Janice Davies, ?, ?, ?, ?, ?, ?, ?, ?, ?, Daphne Watts, ?; third row: all unknown; second row: ?, ?, ?, ?, Barbara Frost, ?, ?, Phyllis Fielding, Sylvia Miners, Diana Lee, Valerie Couch, ?, ?, Miss Violet Hookins, Miss C. Williams, Mrs Sumner (née Weir), Miss C. Weir, Miss M. Agnew, Miss O'Hara, Miss Leppington, ?, ?, Margaret Lewis, Julie Dakin, Mollie Clothier, ?, Elizabeth Burroughs, Cherry Bryant, ?, Sally Clarke, Mary Walker; front: ?, ?, ?, ?, ?, ?, ?, ?, ?, ?, ?, Frances Smith, ?, ?, ?, ?, ?, ?, Josie Bolz, ?, ?, ?, ?, ?, ?, ?, ?, ?, ?, ?, ?, ?.

Burton House School Guide Company on the 21st anniversary of their founding.
Left to right, back row: ?, Jean Elmes, ?, ?, Audrey Morgan, ?, ?, ?, ?, ?, Yvonne Davis; front: ?, ?, ?, Brenda Jackson, ?, ?, ?, ?, Marlene Stephens, ?, ?, ?, ?, Mrs Mumner (headmistress), Norma Thomas, ?, ?, ?, ?, ?, ?, ?, ?, ?, Miss Violet Hookins, ?, Miss C. Williams, ?.

The Children's Church, October 1952. Ena Monday founded the Children's Church in September 1942. Ena, known by everyone as Monday, was a Sunday School teacher but wanted to do more than just teach. Together with some members of her previous Sunday Schools, they came up with the idea of an interdenominational children's church, run by and for the children themselves. This was quite a shocking concept at the time. They began by meeting every Sunday morning in Christ Church Parish Hall in Alfred Street. By 1943 there were 50 regular attendees but that year Christ Church Hall was requisitioned for war use. Undefeated, they launched a building fund so that they could have their own church. In June 1946 after three years hard work, they had sufficient money to buy two derelict houses in Swiss Road, which came with an old builder's yard at the rear. Local builder, Arthur Taylor, gave up his spare time and, with the help of the children their church was opened. Pews were rescued from the redundant Wick St Lawrence Methodist Chapel while the choir pews came from another Methodist chapel at Chiltern Polden, as did the pulpit, which had to be cut down to fit. The opening on 29 September 1947 received nationwide publicity and the membership swelled to 100 children, of all ages up to 17.

As well as a Sunday morning service, there were meetings on Sunday evenings at which speakers lectured or Monday gave a short talk. There were three choirs, including a 'Babies' Den Choir' for the under three year olds. The Children's Church has now closed and the building is currently a Bible Study Centre. Monday died aged 94, on 29 December 1989.

Left to right, back row: ?, Pamela Wagner; front: ?, Alan Merrick, ?, ?, ?.

The Mayor's Christmas Party at the Winter Gardens, Weston-super-Mare, 1952. A ventriloquist entertains the children, many of whom are the offspring of ex-servicemen as the United Services Club Sports Committee held their party in conjunction with the Mayor's event. The mayor at this time was Alderman R.W. Brown. Could this be the same Robert Willcox Brown who was a well-known studio photographer in Weston? His studio was in High Street, Weston. The two children in the centre facing the camera are Richard Craddock (in a dark waistcoat) and his brother Robert (in the checked waistcoat).

St Paul's Church Cub & Scout Group, 1954.
Left to right, second row: ?, ?, ?, Phyllis Craddock, "Stoker" White, ?, Rev. Harrison (Vicar of St Paul's Church), ?, ?, ?, ?, ?.
The boy seated in the front row, fourth from the right is Richard Craddock.

Fancy Dress Parade on Bournville Recreation Ground, 1955. Alan Richardson is dressed up as a Swiss Mountaineer with the Placard "I'm Off, Gotta Find the Summit Talks". The Geneva Summit in Switzerland was held in July 1955 to try and reduce international tensions, which were at their peak around this time. It was a meeting of "The Big Four" powers of the time – President Eisenhower of the United States, Prime Minister Anthony Eden of the United Kingdom, Premier Nikolai A. Bulganin of the Soviet Union, and Prime Minister Edgar Faure of France and was the first conference between the USA and Russia. No important agreements were forged, but the meeting eased some Cold War tensions.

Alan Richardson again, this time dressed up to publicise the "Mind that Child" road safety campaign, 4 September 1956. By the end of the three-month nationwide campaign, 41 fewer children had been killed and more than 700 fewer injured than in the same period the previous year. The campaign was focused on two issues – to remind motorists to be more careful around pedestrians and children, and to increase the numbers of children taking the cycling proficiency tests. These were introduced by the Royal Society for the Prevention of Accidents in 1947. The cycling training had always been a summer event, but was introduced throughout the whole year. It was felt that as a proficient cyclist, a child would become a safer pedestrian and a better driver in due course.

Bournville Infant School, mid 1950s. This school was opened in Selworthy Road on 17 February 1941. It had been completed earlier but the opening was delayed due to the outbreak of war. It was very advanced for its time, even including special heated drying rooms for wet coats. The first head teacher was Mr Knight. Children started in the nursery at the age of three and stayed until they were eight when they moved on to Bournville Junior School. The Infant School was closed for a short time between 30 June and 6 July 1942 so it could be used as an emergency feeding centre after the major bombing raids that month. Their caretaker, Bob Payne, risked his own life to rescue four people and recover one body from a building demolished by a bomb. For this heroism he was later awarded the British Empire Medal.

In 2009 work began on a new £9.7 million singe-storey building to amalgamate both Bournville Infant and Junior Schools. Aside from catering for 420 pupils, it will also provide rooms for a nursery, community facilities and the police. It is being built on the school playing fields. When completed the old buildings will be demolished and that site will become the new playground and playing field. The boy facing the camera in the chair-rocker to the left is Alan Richardson.

St John's Ambulance Cadets carnival float, 14 May 1951. They are pictured outside Emmanuel Church in Oxford Street before parading through Weston to Worle Recreation Ground. The lorry was lent by Slocombe & Hall, Builders' Merchants from 49 Stafford Road. At the front on the right is Cadet Officer, Gerald Richardson.

Collecting for the St John's Ambulance Brigade on Weston seafront, 1950s. On the left is Gerald Richardson, with a one of the St John's nurses. The barrel organ was a regular feature of their street collections as it attracted welcome attention.

Gerald Richardson in the uniform of a St John's Ambulance driver, on the roof of the St John's Ambulance Headquarters in Oxford Street, Weston, 1950s. The Town Hall can be seen on the right.

St John's Ambulance staff, with their two vehicles at the Brigade headquarters in Oxford Street, Weston-super-Mare, late 1950s. The local branch of the St John's Ambulance was formed by John Cox in 1906 with just a handful of volunteers and a hand stretcher on two wheels. They bought their first motor ambulance during the First World War, when it was mainly used to transport wounded soldiers from the station where they arrived by train, to the Red Cross hospital at Ashcombe House. Once again in the Second World War they were called on day and night, to administer first aid and transport the injured and sick especially during the bombing raids. In 1963 County Ambulance Services were formed to take over from the voluntary brigades and they moved from this base in Oxford Street to a new ambulance station in Drove Road. This is still use today by the Great Western Ambulance Service NH Trust.
Left to right: ?, Gerald Richardson, Victor Belcher.

The St John's Ambulance Headquarters in Oxford Street, 1950s. The man on the left is Fred Cooper.

Scene from the play *Separate Tables* by Terence Rattigan, performed by the Red Triangle Players at the Playhouse Theatre, April 1958. *Separate Tables* is a pair of one-act plays exploring the lives of a disparate group of guests at a seaside hotel out of season.
Left to right: Nora Dare-Frampton as Mrs Railton-Bell, Elizabeth Barthwick as Lady Matheson, Jeanne Hillman as the maid Doreen, Joyce Collins as Pat Cooper, Ula Gilbert as Sybil Railton-Bell, Doris Foreman as the maid Mabel.

Doris Foreman as Jack in the British Legion pantomime, *Jack and the Beanstalk* at Knightstone Theatre, 1953.

The British Legion Pantomines are legendary in local theatrical circles. They were performed between 1935 and 1958 and involved large numbers of local people. They originated just before the First World War by the Dimolines as private shows for friends and family. Some twenty years later Victor Dimoline and Wilfred Roe, who had both performed in these shows, thought it would be good to produce just one more for old times sake. Alec Nicholls became business manager and approached the British Legion to see if they would like any profits of the show to be donated to them. The pantomime opened in Knightstone Theatre in 1935 and was such a resounding success they were asked back the following year, and then the year after that and the rest, as they say, was history.

In 1939, the outbreak of the Second World War resulted in the shows being suspended for the duration. However, as soon as peace returned plans were made to resume them. The next performance was Robinson Crusoe in 1946, when St Dunstan's Homes for the Blind was added to the British Legion as a recipient of any profits. The scripts were often doctored to bring in local references but everything had to be approved by the Lord Chamberlain's Office who was responsible for censorship of all shows.

Auditions began around August and were advertised in the local press as open to anyone. Rehearsals began in September. The shows may have been performed by amateurs, but amateurism was not acceptable. One young cast member remembered being kept at rehearsals until past midnight. At one time the rehearsals were held on the top floor of the Gas Company Stores in Burlington Street, currently North Somerset Museum. The whole production utilised local people and services. Scenery was provided by the Fredericks' Studios of Weston. Dancers came from local schools, notably the Mavdor Troupe and later, the Alexander School of Dance.

The excellent reputation of the British Legion Pantomines spread far and wide and tickets sold out very quickly indeed. They began with three evening performances, but these soon grew to ten days of evening shows and matinees. In 1949, police had to control the crowds and close Knightstone Causeway, due to the numbers of people who had come hoping for cancellations.

By 1958, the producers, actors and directors were getting on in years and younger performers didn't want to do pantomime. That year saw the final production – *Babes in the Wood*.

British Legion Pantomine, *Jack & the Beanstalk* with Leslie Powell as Dame Durdan and Adrian Harper as King Stoney-Broke, 1953. Leslie Powell was well-known as an ex-member of the Stars In Battledress who had entertained the troops during the Second World War. While those performing with Ensa were still civilians and therefore were restricted in where they could go, Stars in Battledress were recruited from among serving soldiers, sailors and airmen, and could be sent anywhere. It was a way to get concert parties to entertain troops at the front line. Other famous names who served in this way include Spike Milligan, Jon Pertwee and Frankie Howerd.

Weston-super-Mare Operatic Society Dinner, 1958. Left to right, on the top table: Frank Cantell (BBC Conductor), Doris Foreman, Reginald Thomas, Dorothy Champion, Len John, Pauline John, Lew Stuckey, Pam Stuckey, Leon Godby, Betty Harper, Adrian Harper, Mrs Dennis, Leonard Dennis (of the BBC).

Victorian Weston had a host of talented residents whose dramatic and musical talents were normally displayed only at home or on the occasional charity evening performance, but in 1866 the Elocution & Harmonic Society was formed to teach men to speak properly and women to sing. Thirteen years later the Weston Histrionic Club was formed. This was a largely Temperance Society club, performing weekly concerts where the audience also got a free coffee and a bun! Ironically the performances were usually in a room in a public house.

Throughout the nineteenth century, the only one proper public venue for concerts was the Assembly Room in West Street. So the opening of Knightstone Theatre in 1902 was a great step forward. This was enhanced further when the Grand Pier Pavilion opened in 1904. Weston Operatic Society was formed in 1908 and from that beginning, all other drama and musical groups emerged, very often over disagreements over what to put on!

For example, it was a few disenchanted members of the Operatic Society who formed Weston Dramatic Society, to produce more serious works. From that grew the Red Triangle Players backed by the YMCA. The one unifying event for all the societies were the British Legion Pantomimes, presented at Knightstone Theatre every year between 1935 and 1958, except during the Second World War. They held open auditions so a wide range of talents could be enrolled.

After the War a second theatre became available (the Grand Pier Pavilion had burned down in 1930) when the Playhouse opened in High Street in 1946. Around the same time the Alexandra Players split to form the Wayfarers. In the 1950s almost every club put on their own shows, from the Women's Institutes to the youth clubs. The following decade was probably the heyday of local amateur theatrical groups. The Operatic and Dramatic Societies, Red Triangle Players and Wayfarers all put on two shows every year and The College Players, formed from Technical College Students, had a remarkable run of successes. The fire that destroyed The Playhouse in 1964 created a hiatus in this run and when the new Playhouse opened, the economics were never quite as favourable towards amateur productions.

Red Triangle Players, 1957. This Cabaret entitled 'Arty Laughter',was performed at the YMCA Theatre in the High Street, Weston. Left to right: Wilfred Fredericks, Leslie Scamp, Doris Foreman, Don Harrisson, Kathleen Warren, Don Charsley, Mike Reasons, Fred Astill, Ann-Marie Medland, Peter Rose, Ann Wordman.

Weston Operatic Society's production of *The White Horse Inn* at Knightstone Theatre, October 1957. It was produced by Leon Godby. Set in Northern Austria, this show was memorable for the on-stage appearance of a goat, kindly lent by RAF Locking, whose mascot it was. Left to right: Bill Jacobs, Jeanne Hillman, Sidney Martin, Joyce Rainbow, Pat Clair, Doris Foreman, Lou Stuckey, Eric Joy, David Palmer, ?.

A scene from *Call me Madam* at the Knightstone Theatre, October 1956. This was a joint production by Weston Operatic Society and the Red Triangle Players and was the first modern musical they performed. The story revolves around Washington hostess, Sally Adams, who becomes a US ambassador to a European Grand Duchy. The scene shows Margaret Minifie as Princess Maria and David Palmer as Kenneth Gibson. At this time David Palmer was in the RAF, based at Locking and this was his first ever musical. He later went on to join the D'Oyley Carte Company as a professional singer.

Another scene from *Call me Madam* at the Knightstone Theatre, October 1956. The picture shows Doris Foreman from the Operatic Society as Sally Adams and Leslie Scamp from the Red Triangle Players as Cosmo Constantine. The producer was Wilfred Fredericks.

Weston Operatic Society, pictured outside their rehearsal hall at Walliscote School, 1957.
Left to right, back row: ?, ?, ?, John Tasker, ?, ?, ?, ?, ?, ?, Eric Joy, ?, ?, ?; Third row: ?, ?, John Collins, ?, Joyce Rainbow, ?, ?, ?, ?, ?, Cora Llewellyn, ?, ?, ?, ?, ?; Second row: ?, ?, ?, ?, Leslie Fursland (founder member and Chairman), Lou Stuckey (later chairman), Leon Godby (Musical Director), ?, Jessica Hillman (Pianist), ?, ?; front: Heather Collins, ?, Margaret Minifie, Sylvia Tryhorn, ?, Jeanne Hillman, ?, Doris Foreman, ?.

Worlebury Golf Club, 1952. Worlebury Golf Club was founded in 1908 by a group of local businessmen, headed by Henry Butt, who later became Weston's first Mayor in 1937. He set up Worlebury Club because two years earlier he had applied for membership of Weston Golf Club and been turned down on the grounds that the club was for professional people, not tradespeople. Butt gradually purchased sufficient land at Worlebury and employed a professional golfer, Harry Vardon and his two brothers, to design the course. Nine holes opened on 30 May 1908, with a further nine holes added the following year. Two years later a clubhouse was built with the first club captain, the Reverend J. Doorbar of Kewstoke, appointed in 1912. During the Second World War the course and clubhouse were used by the US soldiers that were stationed throughout the town in the run-up to D-Day. Worlebury and the woods were used to hide vehicles and equipment. One soldier unfortunately left a burning cigarette on a chair and the resulting fire nearly destroyed the clubhouse! By the mid 1950s the club was almost bankrupt, but their fortunes began to improve. The shareholders donated their shares, making it into a Members Club in 1972. It is now one of the few Golf Clubs in the area that owns its own course and clubhouse, the latter being rebuilt in the late 1990s, with nearly 600 members. The man on the right in the middle row is George "Bunt" Bryan. Sixth from the left in the back row is Lloyd Jenkins and second from the left at the front is Dick Farr.

Mayoral Reception and Ball at the Winter Gardens, 1956.
Left to right: ?, George Bryan, ?, Muriel Bryan, Cllr Robert Ivens (Mayor), ?, Derek Palmer, ?, Sybil Rich (?)

Weston-super-Mare Rugby Football Club Annual Dinner, 1950s.

Golden Wedding Anniversary celebration for Winifred and William "Pat" Farr, December 1958. This was a family party held at the Berni Royal Hotel (now the Royal Hotel) in South Parade. The Farrs owned the well-known fish and chip shop in St James Street and were one-time winners of the National Fish Fryers Competition.

Surveyor's and Auctioneer's Dinner Dance, Weston-super-Mare, 1950s.
At the table, far side, left to right, George "Bunt" Bryan, Muriel Bryan, ?, ?; near side: Margaret Burgess, ?, ?, ?.

John, Jenny and Jane Bryan in the garden of their home at 5 Eastfield Gardens, Weston-super-Mare, c.1950.

Weston-super-Mare Central Skittle League Annual Dinner, Friday 28 May 1954. This was the third annual dinner and dance held by the group. They are pictured in the Winter Gardens Pavilion. Dinner consisted of tomato soup, cold boiled ham with mixed salad and creamed potatoes, apricot Melba, cheese, biscuits and coffee, after which there was dancing to music from George Locke and his band. Those standing at the top table include Mayoress, Mrs Margaret J. Grey and the League President Councillor L. Holtby with his wife.

Weston-super-Mare Central Skittle League Fourth Anniversary Dinner Dance at the Winter Gardens Pavilion, 27 May 1955. Nine cups and awards were presented. League winner of Division 1 was the Unionist Club. League winner of Division II, the "Knuts". The Councillor Holtby Knock-out Cup went to the "Wanderers". The B Trapnell Knock-out Cup was won by Bristol Aircraft Company's "Bs". The Division 1 Front Pin was awarded to the Bournville "A's". The Division II Front Pin went to St Andrew's Bowling Club. The George Davis Cup went to Services "B", the Home and Away Spares to J. Coole and the Eight Highest Away Averages to J. Tucker.

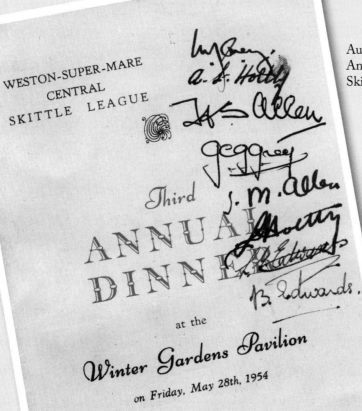

Autographed programme and menu for the Third Annual Dinner of the Weston-super-Mare Central Skittle League, 1954.

Weston-super-Mare Central Skittle League cup winners, 1955.

Division I
League Winners	Unionist Club
Runners-up	Bournville "A's"

Division II
League Winners	The "Knuts"
Runners-up	Boro' Sports "A's"

Councillor Holtby Knock-out Cup
Winners	The "Wanderers"
Runners-up	Bournville "A's"

B. Trapnell Knock-out Cup
Winners	B.A.C. "B's"
Runners-up	The "Knuts"

Division I—Front Pin
Winners	Bournville "A's"
Runners-up	The "Stragglers"

Division II—Front Pin
Winners	St. Andrew's Bowling Club
Runners-up	Bournville "B"

George Davis Cup
Winners	Services "B"
Runners-up	Holtby & Dudman

Home and Away Spares
	J. Coole
	St. Andrew's Bowling Club

Eight Highest Away Averages
	J. Tucker
	Bournville "A"

Whitecross Townswomen's Guild Christmas Party at the Town Hall, Weston, 1950s. This branch of the Townswomen's Guild was founded in 1952. Centre front is chairman, Mrs L. F. Hunt. The party was organised by Mrs Johnson and the Entertainments Committee, with Mr and Mrs Buckley as joint Masters of Ceremony. Entertainment was provided by the recently formed choir, conducted by Mrs Shore. The national movement of Townswomen's Guilds was formed when women first won the right to vote in the 1920s, with the aim of educating women about good citizenship.

Whitecross Townswomen's Guild Christmas Pantomime at the Friends Meeting House in Oxford Street, Weston-super-Mare, 1950s. Here the Ugly Sisters are dancing at Cinderella's Wedding Ball. The whole production was presented in mime, under the direction of Mrs Harris and Miss Miles, while Mrs Harris narrated the story to synchronise with the miming. Music was provided by the Salvation Army Tambourine Band, and games, competitions and supper completed the evening.

Raymond Goold, aged seven, at the piano in the Odeon Cinema, Weston, 1950. Raymond was the son of local estate agent, auctioneer and last Mayor of Weston Borough Council, Vernon Goold. Here, he was performing at a charity concert. Ray began to play classical music whilst in the local Youth Orchestra. He later developed an interest in jazz when he met Frank Brooker. He changed over from the piano to the double bass and has since toured the USA and is currently well known on the European Jazz Festival circuit.

Vernon Goold with his son Raymond, on Knightstone Causeway, 1950. Vernon was a well-known local estate agent and auctioneer, with offices in Orchard Street, Weston. In 1973/74 Vernon was the last Mayor of Weston Borough Council before Local Government Reorganisation created the new County of Avon.

Winners of the annual Talent Contest held at the Winter Gardens, 1952. The child sitting on the grand piano with the teddy bear is Carole Tremlin. She was the overall winner that year for which she won a prize of £1. Her mother used the money to buy a special vase which she still treasures.

Tony Tremlin (left) and his cousin Mike Vizard of Weston, both aged around eight. They were photographed while on a trip to London to visit The Festival of Britain exhibition, 1951.

The Salvation Army Songsters in the Citadel in Carlton Street, 1954. The Citadel was built in 1881. Among the people pictured are Annie Cope, her two adult daughters Joyce Pearce and Ivy Cope, Mrs Beatrice Bressington and her daughter, Beatrice Tremlin. Mrs Bressington and her husband were the caretakers for the Citadel and lived up a lane off Carlton Street in Shaddicks Cottages, together with their

daughter and son-in-law, Beatrice and Ronald Tremlin. They were all re-housed in the mid 1950s, when the area was scheduled for demolition and redevelopment. Beatrice Tremlin died in the summer of 1958 after a long illness, and her husband remarried, to Ivy Cope. This Citadel was closed in October 1999 after the central heating failed and the building was condemned. It was demolished two years later and replaced on the same site with a new £830,000 headquarters, designed as both a church and community centre, with an 80-seat worship hall, another smaller hall, offices, showers and a snack bar area. It was opened on the 17 January 2004 by the territorial commander, Alex Hughes with a ceremony, at which 85 year old Joyce Pearce was fêted as the oldest and longest serving member. Joyce was the first person to enter the new building, accompanied by the youngest member, eight year old Ryan Windget.

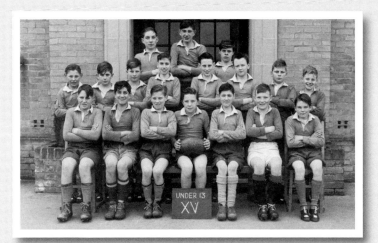

Worle School under 13 Rugby Fifteen, 1953/54
Left to right, back row: Ronald Gill, John Riden,
Peter Robinson;
centre: Roy Wilmot, Richard Burgess, Alan Smithers,
? , Malcolm Venn, Mike Bubear, Peter Fry, Dermot
O'Connel; front: ? , Tony Counsell, ? , David Moxey,
Peter Hoddinot, Graham Hunt, Terry Widlake.

Class 4A, Worle School, 1957.
Left to right, back row: Susan Wright, Alan Denny, Alison Hammond, Christopher Ashmore, Malcolm Venn, Terry Alan,
Brian Bond, Marion Jones; centre: Vicky Venn, Jean Barnes, Margaret Wilcox, Susan Walters, Tony Bowerman, Edwina
Sorbie, Diane Cooper, Elizabeth Vowles, Anita Bowering, Annette Porter; front: Margaret Smith, Gillian Palmer, Gillian
Stabbins, Isobel Hooper, Mr Brown (teacher), Trevor Jarvis, Raymond Munden, John Hodgson, Paul Bishop.

Worle County Secondary School was established in 1940 in Spring Hill, in what is now St Martin's Junior School. The
school opened under headmaster Mr Bisgrove, with 133 pupils, including evacuees from three London schools.
To add authenticity to domestic science classes, which were only open for girls, Worle School had what was known as The
Flat. There was a bedroom, bathroom, lounge and kitchen each fully kitted out like a normal home. For five days, two girls
at a time were expected to spend their school hours cleaning the flat, cooking all their meals and washing bed linen etc. They
would also entertain friends and staff, including the Headmaster. The Flat was later converted into additional classrooms as
school numbers grew. While the girls were learning to run a home, the boys were taught metal work, woodwork and
gardening. The latter was a reminder of the war years when food production was so important. Part of the school grounds
were turned into a vegetable garden, with the produce used in the school kitchens.

In 1971 the whole country's education was reorganised along comprehensive lines. Worle Secondary School became Worle
Comprehensive and moved into a new building in Redwing Drive and the old school buildings in Spring Hill became St
Martins Primary School.

Invoice from Stokes'
Motors, 1 November 1958.
The car showrooms in
Orchard Street were on
the west side, near to the
junction with the
Boulevard. They were
still operating from the
same premises well into
the 1970s.

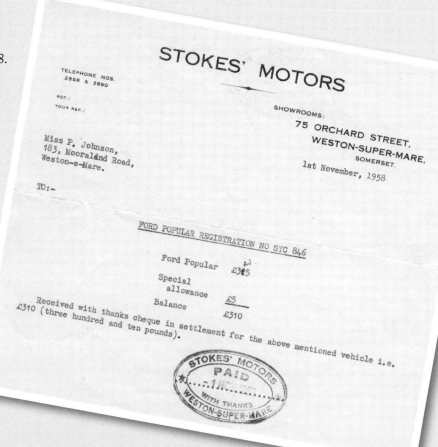

Invoice from Payne's Furnishing Shop for reupholstering a bed settee and large wing chair, 15
April 1955. The shop was on the eastern side of Whitecross Road near to the junction with
Severn Road.

The 1960s

It is said of the 1960s that if you remember them you weren't there! This was the decade of drugs, drink and rock and roll as pop culture came into fashion! The Beatles played in Weston for a week in 1963, as did many other up and coming groups, among them the Rolling Stones, Gerry & the Pacemakers and Pink Floyd.

1961 saw the closure of one of the town's oldest industries – the Royal Potteries. Founded in the 1840s, the pottery had been producing bricks, floor and roof tiles and flower pots for export all over the world. Its demise was put down to the rise of the plastic flowerpot. Another long-standing business which closed in the 1960s was Hillman's Iron Foundry in Richmond Street. You can still spot their products all over the town, in the form of drain grills, manhole covers etc.

The following year is probably best remembered by many as being one of the worst winters on record. The Big Freeze began on Boxing Day 1962 with heavy snowfalls across most of southern England. On the night of the 29 December a blizzard swept across the South West and Wales causing snowdrifts up to 6 metres in places, making roads and railways impassable. The snow cut off villages and brought down power lines. As the New Year dawned, another 45cm of snow fell and the country started to freeze with temperatures as low as –22 degrees centigrade. In January 1963 even the sea froze. The ice on the upper reaches of the River Thames was thick enough in some places that people were even driving on it. Icicles hung from many roof gutters, some of them as long as a metre. More snow came in February with a three-day blizzard causing heavy drifting snow in most parts of the country – again up to 6m. Thousands of farm animals died as it became impossible to get fodder to them. With many roads blocked by snowdrifts, coal could not be transported from the mines. Most people relied on coal-fired heating and the fuel shortages and un-insulated homes led to many deaths from hypothermia.

In Weston, bulldozers were used to try and keep the main roads clear, with the surplus snow piled onto the beach. At Uphill, the coffin of Jessie Ellard, one-time manageress of Georges' Restaurant in Weston High Street, had to be transported by sledge for burial at Uphill Old Church. Not until early March did a gradual thaw set in and the snow finally begin to disappear.

In 1963, a brief experiment was tried, using hovercraft to ferry people between Weston and Penarth in Wales. This was not a success and the steamers continued to operate for some years yet.

In 1965 the first shops opened in Dolphin Square, replacing the original vision of a new tower-block hotel, library and town hall. Sadly the homes demolished for the planned scheme could not be replaced and the back wall of Carlton Street car park stands testament to them, with the old fireplaces and doorways still visible. Other new buildings in this decade include St Peter's Church, Worle Library and the Telephone Exchange in the Boulevard. The town also got a new theatre, after the old Playhouse was destroyed by fire in 1964. Buildings lost at this time were St John's School, demolished to make way for Weston College and the Italianate mansion of Villa Rosa in the Shrubbery. These were just the vanguard as a decade of demolition and rebuilding followed in the 1970s.

King Alfred Masonic Lodge Ladies' Night, 1968. The first Masonic Lodge – Athelstan - was founded in Weston-super-Mare in 1868 with 24 members. By the end of the century, membership had grown to such proportions that a second Lodge was proposed. King Alfred Lodge was formed in 1906 with a ceremony at the Assembly Rooms, on the corner of West Street and High Street, followed by a luncheon at the Victoria Hall. Since that time, two further Lodges have been founded – Wessex and Birnbeck. The above photograph was taken in the Centenary Year. The occasion was marked by a Centenary Festival on 9 July 1968. This included a Thanksgiving Service at the Parish Church and a Festival Banquet at the Grand Atlantic Hotel.

Playhouse Theatre poster of the 1960s. This refers to the original Playhouse, converted from the old Market House in the High Street. The market building was redundant and with a few cosmetic changes such as a false ceiling and some hessian drapes along the walls, it became a second theatre for Weston complementing the one at Knightstone. In the early 1960s, the building was extensively modernised and was able to put on a wide variety of entertainment, from ballet and classical music, to drama, farce, comedy and one-man shows. Many major stars of the day trod its boards including Frankie Howerd, Ken Dodd, Bob Monkhouse, Leslie Crowther, Brian Rix, Dickie Henderson and Terry Scott. On the night of 21 August 1964 however, fire broke out and the building was totally destroyed. After much debate as to whether to replace the theatre or rebuild elsewhere, work began on the same site in 1967. The new Playhouse opened two years later and is still in use today.

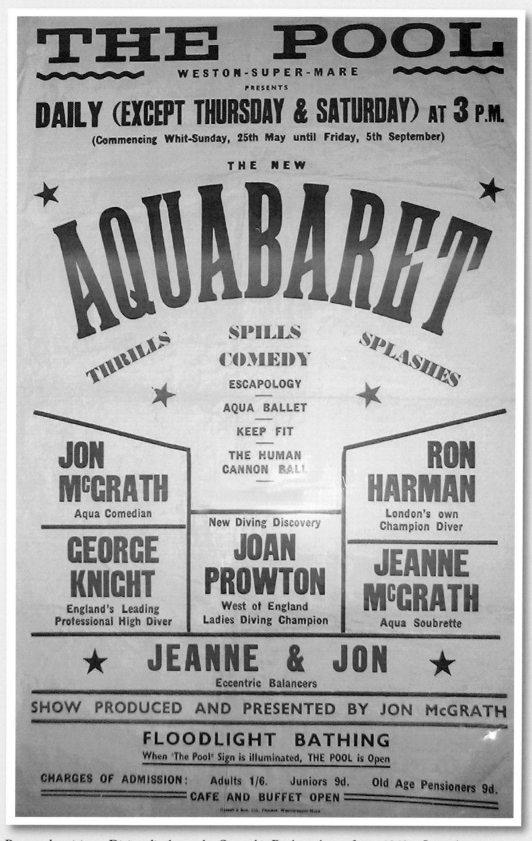

Poster advertising a Diving display at the Open Air Pool on the seafront, 1960s. Special events at the pool were put on regularly during the summers. Jean Overy recalls seeing a demonstration of "log-rolling" by a team of Canadian lumberjacks, as well as diving exhibitions and comic diving displays.

Open Air Pool, 1960s. The spectacular Olympic standard diving stage was one of Weston's most familiar landmarks and frequently featured on advertising posters for the town. As modern health and safety rules were brought in it was felt there wasn't sufficient depth of water under them. Unfortunately the reinforced concrete structure was also beginning to fail so, despite a spirited battle to save it, the stage was demolished in 1982, when the pool was converted into the Tropicana Pleasure Beach.

Scene from the play *Arms & the Man* by the College Players at the Playhouse Theatre, Weston, 1963. This comedy was one of George Bernard Shaw's earliest plays, written in 1894, but set during the 1885 Serbo-Bulgarian War. Left to right: Simon Cord as Petkoff, Anne Abrahams as Louka, Francis Newton as Sergius, Richard (Glyn) Lewis as Nicola.

A Wayfarer's production of *The Gentle Arm* at Weston Playhouse, October 1960. Left to right: George Ramage, Brian Austin, Cynthia Thorne, Mary Mason, Gwen Watson, Noel Pardy.

A summer weekend at the Uphill end of Weston beach, 1963.

Hovercraft on Weston Beach, 1963. P & A Campbell, who operated the Bristol Channel pleasure steamers, briefly trialled a hovercraft service between Penarth and Weston. They used a Westland SRN2 craft, the journey taking 12 minutes and costing £1. It was not a success and the service ran for just the 1963 season. The steamers continued a regular service to and from Birnbeck Pier until 1979. They are now just occasional visitors.

Ernest Tottle (right) with another officer, both of the North Somerset Yeomanry, a local Territorial Regiment on the Beach Lawns. Behind them is the Bus Station. They were tasked to escort the Mayor of Weston, Cllr Harry Allen, at the Dairy Festival, 1960. During World War Two, the Yeomanry fought in the Far East, and Syria. In 1943 they were converted to the Royal Corps of Signals and as such served in the Western Desert, Sicily, Italy, and North West Europe. After the War the Yeomanry became the Armoured Regiment of 16th Airborne Division, joined 44th Royal Tank Regiment to become The North Somerset and Bristol Yeomanry in 1956, and in 1967 merged with The Somerset Light Infantry (TA) to form The Somerset Yeomanry and Light Infantry.

The Dairy Festivals were held annually on the Beach Lawns between 1958 and 1976. They used at attract around 150,000 people to the beauty contests, milking and cookery demonstrations, cattle parades and sheep dog trials.

Pupils and staff from St John's Secondary Modern School, Lower Church Road, Weston, setting off on a trip to Austria, 3 January 1963. The 37 pupils and four teachers, travelled by boat and coach on this eleven-day skiing trip. None of the pupils had ever skied before, aside from a practice run on a dry ski slope. Ironically, this trip was during the coldest winter since 1740 and there was plenty of snow in Weston to ski on, without travelling across Europe. St John's School closed in 1964 and was demolished to make way for Weston Technical College

Left to right: ?, Alan Merrick, Malcolm Bowen, ?, Carol Staples, Janet Powell, Mr Harry Lye (Headmaster), Rickson Hough, ?, Roy Slocombe, Mrs Langstone (teacher), Mr Langstone, Lynda Thomas, Mrs Lye, ?, ?, ?, ?, Shirley Mallet, Carol Davies, ?. Standing on the bottom of the bus steps to the right is David Jones.

Ticket for a Rolling Stones concert at the Odeon Cinema, 1960s. Throughout the 1960s and early 1970s, the Odeon Cinema or Winter Gardens Pavilion played host to many well-known groups such as the Rolling Stones, Pink Floyd, Jethro Tull, Desmond Dekker & the Aces and Georgie Fame & the Blue Flames and, in 1963, the Beatles. The person responsible for the acts at the Winter Gardens was skilled at booking groups just before they became really famous so that they were available and affordable, but by the time they performed in Weston they had become well-known.

Weston-super-Mare ambulance drivers and staff at Drove Road Ambulance Station, c.1966.
Left to right, back row: "Maccy" Melhuish, Tom Holley, Tony Booy, Fred Cooper, Mike Hawkins, Roy Thorne, Keith Bartlett; third row: Dennis Cotgrove, Dave Nock, Kerry Mitchell, Vic Belcher, Derek Jones, Dave Spencer, Len Trowbridge, Danny Brewer, Cecil Balaam;
second row: Brian Parfitt, Charlie Howe, Johnny Davis, L. Osborne, Gerald Richardson, Freddy Norville; front: Gordon Godfrey, ?.

United Services Club members outing, c.1960. The United Services Club was in the Boulevard, where this picture was taken. As its name suggests, it was a social club for members and ex-members of the armed forces. It closed in the 1990s and is now a lap dancing club. The shop to the left was Phillput's Stationers, and is currently a hairdresser's.
Left to right, back row: Gordon Abrey, ?, ?, ?, ?, ?, ?, Frank Galloway. ?, ?, ?, ?, Victor Board, ?, ?, ?, ?, ?, Bill Kennedy, ?, ?, Ken Sullivan, ?, ?, ?, ?, ?, Don Smith, Harry Webber, Jim Usher, ?, Eric Poulson, ?;
Front row: Des Taylor, Ernest Smart, Ernest Reasons, ?, ?, ?, ?, ?, Bill Meakin, ?, ?, Jeff Willingham, Les Kennedy, Fred Kennedy, Ron Lewis, Charlie Banwell, ?, Ron Ellis, Tim Rawlins, ?, Albert Penberthy.
The man on the bus at the middle window is Stan Harris.

Gerald Richardson of 91 Totterdown Road, Weston, prior to receiving the award of Serving Brother of the Order of St John at an investiture in 1963. He is actually dressed in the uniform of the Somerset County Ambulance Brigade in the photograph. It was around this time what the County Ambulance Services were formed to take over from the St John's Ambulance Brigades. Following that reorganisation, the Millar report of 1964 recommended that ambulance services should also provide treatment as well as transporting patients to hospital. As a result of this, ambulance staff began to provide life saving procedures such as bleeding control, neck and back injury care, cardiopulmonary resuscitation and fluid, drug and oxygen therapy.

Christmas Lunch organised by the Weston St John's Football & Social Club, 1965. This annual event catered for over 140 older people at the Winter Gardens Pavilion. After the lunch there was community singing and other entertainment in the Pergola Room, followed by a buffet tea. The Mayor, Alderman Boyd, is on the top table with Alderman Haskins third from the right. It was at this particular event that the announcement was made that Weston St John's AFC had acquired the old Windwhistle Inn in Chaucer Road, Bournville. They planned to convert it into club and committee rooms and a day centre for elderly people. Once open, fund-raising would continue so that a gymnasium and training facilities could also be provided on the site.

Some of the players and committee members of Weston St John's Football Club, working to convert the old Windwhistle Inn into a social club and committee rooms, 1966. It was a huge project carried out entirely by volunteers, who spent many months painting, re-wiring, decorating and even replacing roof tiles and window glass, all in their spare time.
Left to right: Ken Mugglesworth (general secretary), Phil Bruton, Alan Richardson, Eddy Davis (sports secretary), Jim Bruton (chairman), Jack Moore (treasurer) and Gerald Richardson.

More volunteers working to convert the old Windwhistle pub into the new Social Club, 1966. Mrs E. Davis, M. Muggleworth and Margaret Richardson (social chairman) clean up some the chairs for the new centre.

Players and committee members of the Weston St John's AFC, in the grounds of the old Windwhistle Inn in Chaucer Road, Bournville, Weston, which they were converting into a club house, committee room and social club, 1966. The building behind them is a block of flats.
Left to right, back row: Pete Jefferson, Simon Mugglesworth, Molly Mugglesworth, Eddy Davis, Ken Mugglesworth; front: Dave Pigott, Jim Bruton, Alan Richardson, Margaret Richardson (Alan's mother), Jack Moore, Nigel Bruton.

Margaret Richardson of 91
Totterdown Road, Weston, 1965.
Mrs Richardson was head of the
Social Committee of Weston St
John's AFC as well as working at a
local pharmacy. She spent three
evenings week helping in the
canteen at the Bournville
Community Hall, where social
activities for the elderly were run
throughout the year. Margaret was
the wife of Gerald Richardson and
mother to Alan Richardson (see
pages 66 and 94).

Weston Operatic Society cast members from the musical *Annie Get Your Gun*, pictured behind the theatre at
Knightstone, Weston-super-Mare, 1962. Left to right: Stan Bailey as Charlie Davenport, Lillian Bailey as
Dolly Tate, Don McGregor as Colonel William Cody (Buffalo Bill).

Weston-super-Mare Operatic Society Committee members, April 1966.
Left to right, back row: Len John (Secretary), Peter Brewer, Brian Saunders, Eric Joy, Bill Leonard, Stan Bailey;
Front row: Doris Foreman, Lou Stuckey (Chairman), Jessica Hillman (pianist), Wilfred Roe (President), Dorothy Champion, Tom Sherman, Heather Collins.

John Bryan working as a deckchair attendant during his summer holiday from university, c.1960.

Milkman Ronald Tremlin, with his float, parked outside his house in Martindale Road where he and his family moved to in 1959. Ronald began working for Weston Farmers in the 1950s, staying with the dairy until about 1965. His round was the town centre, including the High Street, the Central GPO Sorting Office by the Winter Gardens and the old hospital in the Boulevard. He was a very well known and popular local 'Milko' and his children Carole and Tony often went on the round with him during the school holidays.

Members of Weston Cricket Club, pictured at the Recreation Ground in Drove Road, c.1962.
Left to right, back row: ?, Ray Phillpott, Roy Porter, John Worrall, ?, John Holland, Derek Stenner, ?, ?, Doug Atwell, Mr Stephenson, Derrick Minifie, Mr Reasons, Roy Davidson, Reg Popham, Derek Hucker, Bob Hedges; centre: Adrian Gillette, Tony Webb, Mike Hughes, ?, Brent Twort, Roger Webber; front: Derek Patch, Mike Fox.

Invoice for new Morris Mini saloon, purchased from Devonshire Road Garages by Miss Johnson of Moorland Road in 1964.

The 1970s

At the beginning of the 1970s, parts of Weston still stood unchanged from decades previous, but this was all to change as many well-known buildings were pulled down to be replaced with apartment blocks – the preferred type of housing at this time. Etonhurst, Kingsholm and Glentworth Hall were all demolished, despite often heated battles to save them. Other historic buildings lost include the Plough Hotel in Regent Street, The Albert Memorial Hall next to Emmanuel Church and The Lodge in Bristol Road, once home to Lord Cavan. Weston Civic Society was formed in 1976 to raise awareness and appreciation of the beauty and elegance of Weston's Victorian landscape in the hope fewer buildings would fall to developers' plans. One building saved was the Gaslight Company Workshops and Stores in Burlington Street, which was purchased by the local authority to be turned, in an award-winning conversion, into a new home for the Museum. At the time of writing however, this unique building is sadly under threat of closure and sale in the current round of local authority budget cuts. If this goes ahead, it will be a great loss to the town and its heritage.

In 1974 Weston Borough Council became a casualty of the changes to local government. Chunks of Somerset, Bristol and Gloucestershire were taken to form a new County of Avon. Within the new county, the District of Woodspring was created, which included Weston and the surrounding areas up to Pill, and across to Blagdon.

Many private schools, of which there were once so many in the town, also closed around this period, including La Retraite School for Girls and St Peter's School for Boys. Both buildings, in South Road and at the end of Shrubbery Avenue respectively, were again demolished for new housing.

In 1977, the Queen and Prince Philip visited Weston as part of their Silver Jubilee Tour of

Great Britain. Crowds turned out to welcome them and street parties were held for the first time since the Coronation.

The following year Weston-super-Mare became twinned with Hildesheim, a city about 30 kms south of Hanover in Germany. It was a move planned to foster peace and understanding between the two cultures and led to many years of exchange visits between school children, as well as various civic events.

Despite the seeming destruction and demolition, not everything was bad. Throughout most of the 1970s you could still board a plane for a pleasure flight from Weston Airport or a steamer from Birnbeck Pier. Knightstone Theatre was newly refurbished for summer season shows. You could still swim at the Open Air Pool and sit and watch tennis at the Winter Gardens. Weston's first adventure playground was built, on the Bournville and a new Tourist Information Bureau opened on the Beach Lawns.

A Weston-super-Mare Skittles League presentation to Dr Mallen at the Dorville Hotel, 1973. Left to right: Joe Whiting, Mr Whiting, Maria Whiting, Billy Carr, Derek Jenkins, Dr Mallen, Albert Bennett and Steve Bailey Jnr.

The Dorville Hotel was in South Road, on the western corner as it curves back down to Birnbeck Road. It is currently derelict and awaiting redevelopment, probably as flats. Joe died on the 5 March 2003 aged 78 having sold the hotel a few months previously. Maria predeceased him by four years.

Pupils at La Retraite School, 1971. This was the year the school closed for good, and these were the last pupils to be taught there. Some transferred to La Retraite at Burnham on Sea, whilst others moved to other private schools.

Stagehands at the Christmas production of *Cinderella* at the Playhouse Theatre, Weston, January 1975.
Left to right, back row: Bob Varcoe (Stage Manager), Sue Donkin (props), Tony Blizzard (Assistant Stage Manager);
third row: Dave Clothier, Norman Trenner, Bernie Watts; second row: Brian Austin, Jill Tucker, Jill Miles; front: Phil Day,
Colin Love (electrics).

The Red Triangle Players production of *The Insect Play,* March 1974. This was staged at the College Theatre in Knightstone Road. This three-act political satire was written by Czech playwright Karel Capek – the man who first coined the word "Robot" in another of his plays. Left to right: Brian Austin, Steve Baker, Gill Young, Sue Donkin, John Stewart, Mike Chew, David Battersby, Annemarie Austin, Annette Oxley, Stephie Read, Mike Usher, Penny Broomhall, Jackie Jackson, Bryn James, Jack Donkin, Jeannie Hillman, Cary Watts.

A Theatre in the Wood production of the fifteenth century French comedy, *The Eel Pie & the Cheese Tart*, 1973. Left to right: Barbara Smith, Gill Cree, ?, Brian Austin, John Butler and Mike Chew. Producer Keith Clark is in the background.

HM The Queen and HRH the Duke of Edinburgh, in Weston as part of the Silver Jubilee Tour
of Britain, 1977. Over 2000 Cubs, Scouts, Brownies and Guides were at the railway station to
greet the Royal couple when the train arrived at 3.52pm on Monday 8 August 1977. The Queen
and Prince Philip were greeted by Woodspring District Council Chief Executive, Robert Moon
and Chairman, Cllr Haskins, together with their wives, before driving along Station Road,
Walliscote Road, Oxford Street and Beach Road to the Beach Lawns. Once there, the Vice
Chairman of the Council, Cllr James Dickson, presented Cllr Doris Edwards (Town Mayor),
Valerie Coates (Mayoress), Jerry Wiggin MP, Cllr David King (Chairman of the Woodspring
Group of the Avon Local Councils Association) and Mrs King, Cllr Thomas Sturgess (Chairman
of Clevedon Town Council) and Mrs Sturgess, Cllr Barry Clothier (Chairman of Nailsea Town
Council) and Mrs Clothier and Cllr Morgan Iles (Chairman of Portishead Town Council) and
Mrs Iles. Miss Celina Haskins, aged eight, presented a bouquet to the Queen, after which a
number of local youth voluntary groups such as the Red Cross, Boys' Brigade, Young Farmers etc,
put on a variety of displays and demonstrations. The Queen and the Duke of Edinburgh left
Weston at 4.30pm to drive to Avonmouth West Dock to board HMY *Britannia*.

Petrina Tottle of the Third Weston Guides receiving the Queen's Guide Award from Guide Captain, Beryl Hughes, at a ceremony at Milton Methodist Church Hall, January 1977. This is the highest award members can work towards in Guiding. It is based around personal challenge and split into five areas - service in guiding, outdoor challenge, personal skill development, community action and residential. For her Service in Guiding section, 14 year old Petrina chose work with the Brownies, acting as Pack Leader. Many of her Brownies were also at the presentation.

Inspecting the silver cups at the Annual General Meeting of Weston Swimming Club, 1973. They are laid out ready to be awarded to the winners.
Left to right: Mr E.J. Doust (Club Secretary), Mr E.M. Rake (President), Mike Heath (Chairman), Douglas Coles, Mrs Page (of Page's Leather Shop in the High Street), Peter Tottle.

The opening of the new Weston St John's Football Club, 1970s. Left to right: ?, Jerry Wiggin MP, George Smith (President), Margaret Richardson (Social Chairman), Lou Langdon, Jim Bruton (Chairman).

Pupils from the Alexander School of Dancing perform at Weston Hospital Fête, 1979. This was held in the grounds of the Royal Hospital in Beach Road. This was originally built as the Royal West of England Sanatorium in 1868, taking convalescent patients from Birmingham. It was closed in 1986 when the new hospital at Uphill opened and has subsequently been converted into housing.

Somerset County Ambulance driver Gerald Richardson plays Santa Claus at a Christmas Day visit to patients at Drove Road Hospital, 1979. This was a regular annual event by Ambulance staff, who were based next to this 38-bed Geriatric Hospital in Drove Road. Like the other hospital buildings scattered throughout the town, Drove Road closed in 1986 when the current hospital opened, bringing all services under one roof.

The Committee and members of the Bournville & District Social Club at their annual Christmas Party, held at the Webbington Hotel, 14 December 1975. The man in the dark suit and tie, just behind the head of the man lying down, is Alan Wells, the proprietor of the Webbington. Next to him in a pinafore dress is Margaret Richardson, Social Chairman of the club.

Jenny Schmeidel (left) and her sister Jane Paterson, with Jane's son, John and daughters Tessa and Clare. Jenny and Jane are outside the home of their parents, Muriel and George "Bunt" Bryan, at 8 Beaconsfield Road, Weston, 1978.

Formal Supper to mark the Dissolution of Weston Borough Council, 27 March 1974. Following the supper, there was dancing to Roy Harris and his band. Local Government Reorganisation rearranged county boundaries in many parts of the country and locally, parts of Somerset, Gloucestershire and Bristol were taken to form a new County of Avon. This was divided into administrative areas among which Weston formed part of the District of Woodspring. Left to right: ?, Valerie Couch, ?, ?, Mrs Brewer, Hilda Goold (Mayoress), May Dickson, Mrs Nicholls.

Pilot and aerial photographer John White with Cllr Vernon and Mrs Hilda Goold, 1974. Vernon Goold was a well-known local estate agent and auctioneer. The picture was taken at Weston Airport, prior to Mr White taking the Goolds on a flight over the town to mark the end of the Borough of Weston, of which Vernon Goold was last Mayor. John White set up the local company West-Air Photography with his sons.

Two pictures of the ladies of the Mendip Singing Group, Weston-super-Mare, 1978.
Left to right, back row: Gwen Taylor, Olwyn Acland, Eileen Cannon, Jean Firrell, Mrs Marsh;
front; ?, Iris Turner, Hilda Goold.

Left to right: Iris Turner, Jean Firrell, Joan Fox, Hilda Goold, Marion Hall, Madge Frankpitt, Gwen Watson, Mrs Marsh MBE, Mrs Price.

The opening of the new housing estate built by Second City at Madam Lane, Worle, 1973. The picture shows the first couples being handed their keys by the Mayor Cllr Vernon Goold and Mayoress Mrs Hilda Goold (left).

Radio One DJ Tony Blackburn makes an appearance at the Top Rank Bingo Hall, Regent Street, 30 August 1973. This building was formerly the Regent Cinema, before being renamed the Gaumont Cinema in 1954. The cinema closed in 1973 and became a Bingo Hall. It has since been demolished. Left to right: Jim West, Tony Blackburn, Vernon Goold, Hilda Goold, Gertrude Butters. Mrs Butters was for many years the main organiser of the town's Summer Carnival.

Junior Red Cross Cadets certificate presentation evening, c.1972. Regular weekly meetings were held on Tuesday evenings in the Red Cross Training and Loan Centre that was in Orchard Street. Yvonne Cresswell recalls that you joined at around seven years old or more and took courses and exams in First Aid, Nursing & Mothercraft. The uniform was a dark skirt or pinafore dress (trousers for the boys), with a white shirt and tie with a Red Cross badge on it and a black beret with a larger badge. As well as the weekly meetings, the cadets did shifts at the First Aid station on the beach during the summer and used to be in attendance at the summer and winter carnivals. After the carnivals everyone went back to the St John's Ambulance Headquarters in Oxford Street where they got a meal. The cadets also used to take part in area and regional competitions where a series of accident scenarios would be set up and teams of four or more from the different Red Cross units would be judged on their response. One event Yvonne remembers was at a big school in the country next to a farm. There were some gruesome farm accident scenarios set up with full realistic stage make-up. A lot of the older girls did go on into nursing but Yvonne came to accept she couldn't cope with blood and later went into museum work. From the left, the officers in the photograph are Miss Avon, Miss Joan Purslow and Mrs Louise Tucker. The District Commander is seated in the centre.

The official Switching On of the Christmas Illuminations in Upper Church Road, Weston, c.1970. This was organised by the Upper Church Road Traders' Association. The area has changed greatly over the last few years and there are now just two shops and one pub left operating.

Upper Church Road Traders' Association summer carnival entry, 1973. The float was on the theme of Dickens and was in three parts. To the left was a scene from *Great Expectations*, in the centre, *Oliver Twist* and to the right and out of the picture was *Pickwick Papers*. Miss Haversham was played by Mrs Cresswell, who ran the Church Road Post Office with her husband, while Oliver was played by her seven year old daughter Yvonne, with the local hoteliers children dressed as Fagin's gang. Following the Carnival, the older participants retired to the Raglan Arms pub to celebrate their win of a trophy!

Woodspring Museum Club summer carnival entry, July 1979. The children of the Saturday morning club were accompanied by Museum staff Geoff Tozer and Sharon Poole. The entry was on the theme of Victorian Seaside Holidays and won the Jeffries Rose Bowl. There was a donkey-chair (pulled by a pony for this occasion), a penny-farthing bicycle (ridden by Geoff Tozer) and walking entries, all in appropriate Victorian seaside dress. The Museum Club ran throughout school term time for children from the age of seven to around 15, meeting every Saturday for events, crafts, talks and demonstrations. It was so popular there was usually a waiting list to join. Some ex-members, like Yvonne Cresswell, went on to have a career in museums.

End of Year exhibition staged by Weston Technical College's art and photographic departments, April 1971. The exhibition hall was in the original School of Science & Art building, constructed in 1893 in Lower Church Road. In 1971 it was the College art department and continued as such until the new University Campus was opened in Loxton Road in 2007. Left to right: Sue Hird, Marion Edwards, Ann McNair.

The 1980s

The 1980s saw the final nail in the coffin of the traditional week or two by the sea in Britain. Foreign package tours came within the reach of many more people and the impact was evident in the closure of many seaside hotels throughout the country. This was not the end of investment though; just that Weston had to reinvent itself as a town that happened to be beside the sea, rather than as a beach resort. The Sovereign Shopping Centre is an example of this. In the late 1980s plans were released for this sweeping new redevelopment, where a large block of the town centre, including the General Post Office, Royal Arcade, Salisbury Terrace and a multi-storey car park were all to be demolished to make way for a modern indoor shopping mall. Similarly the old redundant Goods and Excursion Stations in Locking Road were pulled down to built a large new Tesco supermarket.

In 1980 an extension to the Town Hall was built, on a site once occupied by the Albert Memorial Hall next to Emmanuel Church. And in 1987, following years of campaigning and fundraising, a new hospital opened at Uphill. For the first time this brought all medical services on to one site, where previously they had been scattered throughout the town, with the maternity unit at Ashcombe House, recovery unit at Eastern House and rehabilitation at the Royal Hospital etc. The old buildings were sold with the main hospital in the Boulevard, the Royal Hospital and Eastern House Convalescent Home all converted into housing and Ashcombe House demolished. Also in the Boulevard, the vacant site left by the bombing of the Tivoli Cinema in 1942 was finally redeveloped with flats and a retail unit.

In July 1981 there were celebrations and street parties marking the Royal Wedding between Prince Charles and Lady Diana Spencer. In contrast however, at the end of the year there was widespread coastal destruction as a huge storm hit on 13 December. Much of the promenade was damaged, homes were flooded, especially at Uphill, and the Marine Lake colonnade and

Rozel Bandstand were wrecked beyond repair.

Changes to the seafront included the demolition of the Bus Station and the removal of the iconic diving boards at the Open Air Pool as the latter was modernised and renamed the Tropicana, complete with plastic palm trees and splash pools.

Production of Terence Rattigan's wartime romantic tear-jerker, *Flare Path*, staged by the Red Triangle Players at the Theatre in the Hut, 4 - 8 May 1982.

Rattigan wrote *Flare Path* in 1942 while serving as a gunner on Atlantic U-Boat patrols. The story is about British fighter pilots and the women they love. One of Rattigan's fellow officers during the war, who saw the play when it opened in London was said to have been deeply moved and 'shocked to realize that Rattigan had seen so deeply into us.' Left to right: Pat White, Mike Usher, Joan Fisher, Julian Franks, Brian Austin, Bryn James, Jack Donkin.

Meakin's second-hand furniture store, Baker Street, 1980s. After 66 years of buying and selling anything from household goods to expensive antiques, the business closed in October 1987 when William "Bill" Meakin retired. The yard was a veritable Aladdin's Cave of furniture, china, glass, white goods, pictures and books. The old buildings were demolished in 2004 and Housing Association flats built on the site (see also page 9)

Storm damage to the promenade, 13 December 1981. On the night of 12 December heavy rain and sleet, a fierce westerly gale with wind speeds of up to 95 mph all combined with a high tide, caused a storm surge that wreaked havoc all along the Somerset coast and left a repair bill of some £6 million. Despite weather warnings, no-one expected the level of destruction that was seen the following morning. The worst flooding was along the sea front and at Uphill. The promenade wall was lying as scattered stones, and the colonnade at Marine Lake had collapsed in several places. Coming so close to Christmas heightened the sense of shock, as families had to move into temporary accommodation and faced months of disruption and worry. Amazingly, both the Grand and Birnbeck Piers were undamaged, unlike a similar situation in 1903, when the jetties at Birnbeck were virtually wrecked.

Multi-storey car park, Salisbury Terrace, April 1988. This car park was built in the 1960s on the site of part of the Royal Arcade and properties in White Horse Street behind Marks & Spencer. It was demolished in 1990 as part of the Sovereign Shopping Centre re-development, which included a replacement multi-storey car park on the upper floors.

The remains of the Royal Arcade, April 1988. Originally the Royal Arcade was T-shaped, running from Post Office Road to Regent Street with a branch at right angles to Salisbury Terrace. It was filled with small lock-up shops selling seaside novelties, sweets and jewellery, cafes etc. Part of it was destroyed by a bomb in the Second World War. A small section from the back of Trevor's department store to Post Office Road continued for many years, until it was demolished here, for the Sovereign Shopping Centre development, which opened in 1992. The tall brick building is the back of the General Post Office.

The General Post Office, April 1988. The main part of the building was constructed in 1899 with a dark wood-panelled interior with shining brass fittings. The right hand part of the building was an extension built in 1923 to create a larger sorting office. It was demolished in 1990 and the Sovereign Shopping Centre now stands on the site.

Weston Bay Trefoil Guild. This group was founded in April 1985, specifically for members with special needs. The Trefoil Guild is a world-wide organisation for men and women who have been, or indeed still are, connected with the Boy Scouts and Girl Guides. They offer practical help and support as well as promoting Guide and Scout groups in their local communities.

Among those pictured are Christine Brown, Noelle Schaefer and Pamela Tottle with members Nicola, Diane, Tina, Linda, Annette, Philipa, Jennifer, Iona and Sheila. Their guests are Vera Hinton and Irene Fussell.

In 1983 plans were laid to hold a big reunion of ex pupils and staff of Burton House School, to mark the centenary of its founding in 1886. The main events were a dinner at the Winter Gardens Pavilion on Saturday 5 April. This began with a sherry reception at which the Mayor and Mayoress of Weston, Cllr Leslie Haine and Mrs Freda Haine were among the invited guests. On the Sunday there was a buffet luncheon, followed by a service of thanksgiving at Emmanuel Church in Oxford Street led by the Revd H.L. Franklin, Subdean of Wells Cathedral. Nearly 200 ex-pupils came for the weekend, not just from all over Britain, but even travelling from the USA, Canada, Switzerland and the Channel Islands. Some descendants of the Weir family who established the school, were also able to attend the event.

Left to right, back row: Mavis Fleming (née Dyson), Joan Vowles (née Redding), Betty Haward (née Redding), Pamela Scott (née Armstrong), Barbara Warren (née Fussell), June Scott (née Stickland), Sylvia Cook (née White), Margaret Ekins (née Kimber), June MacDonald (née Jordan); centre: Greta Keeling (née Gardner), Violet Hookins, Connie Williams, Doreen Cooper (née Tolley), Norma Bailey (née Ellery), Wendy Turner (née Ellery), Ena Powell (née Crewe), Ruth Smith (née Lane); front: Helen Rushton (née Gardner), Mary Heigh (née Wood), Joan Player-Mason (née Smith), Jean Ince (née Palmer).

Burton House School reunion, at the sherry reception prior to dinner in the Winter Gardens Pavilion, 5 April 1986. Left to right, back row: Joan Vowles (née Redding), Betty Haward (née Redding), Ena Powell (née Crewe), N. Chammings (née Lane), Dulcie Mathewson (née Higgins), June Scott (née Stickland), Marie House (née Harris), Mary Champion (née Dart), Maureen Cockram (née Champion), Joyce Clapp (née Champion); centre: Elieen Craig (née Hicks), Dorothy Watts (née Forrester), Isobel Welland (née Tolley), Doreen Cooper (née Tolley), Barbara

Warren (née Fussell), Jean Ince (née Palmer), Sylvia Cook (née White), Sybil Rayner (née Blake), Joan Croft (née Rainey); front: Eileen Stevens (née Drew), Joan Player-Mason (née Smith), Mary Mugridge (née Moore).

Burton House School reunion, after dinner in the Winter Gardens Pavilion, 5 April 1986.
Left to right: Verlie Edwards (née Prosser), Christine Kynoch (née Wells), Jennifer Lawrence (née Shroll), J. Rickett (née Haydon), Penny O'Brien (née Shroll), Barbara Bailey (née Phillputt), Susan Poole (née Davies).
All these ex-pupils still live in North Somerset.

Burton House School reunion, at the dinner in the Winter Gardens Pavilion, 5 April 1986.
Left to right: Vera King, Elsie Beaton, Vera Spratt (née Champion). For many years Elsie Beaton was personal secretary to George Thomas, later Viscount Tonypandy and Speaker of the House of Commons.

Winners of a Children's Colouring Competition run by Sam Burge Volvo, 1980s. Sam Burge's chosen charity that year was the Royal National Lifeboat Institution and the prize-winners were treated to a visit to the Lifeboat Station on Birnbeck Pier and a ride round the bay in the lifeboat. Left to right, back row: Richard Spindler (RNLI), Alan Richardson (Sam Burge Volvo), D. Wallace (RNLI), ? (RNLI). The names of the children are not known.

Gerald Richardson on an aeroplane, 1981. A flight from Lulsgate Airport over his old patch was a gift from Gerald's colleagues on his retirement from the Avon County Ambulance Service. He was then the longest-serving ambulance driver in Weston, having covered the area since the early 1950s, first as a St John's Ambulance officer, then for the Somerset and lastly the Avon County Services. Two work colleagues accompanied him on the flight.

Weston Community Health Council Office, Weston General Hospital, mid 1980s. The Community Health Council represented the interests of the public in local healthcare provision. Social Worker, Ann Coia (second from left) and Secretary of the Community Health Council, Edgar Evans (centre), with two French exchange students who were in Weston to see how the National Health Service worked.

Members of the Wayfarers' Drama Group, in the play *Halfway Up the Tree*, 1980s. This comic study of the Parent-Child relationship, its expectations and what happens when it gets turned upside down, was written by the well-known and much loved actor Peter Ustinov. Left to right, back row: ?, ?, Laurie Gillard, Graham Gadd, ?, Ann Coia, Colin Golding, ?; front: John Butler, ?, Joanne James, ?, Barbara James, ?, ?, Jackie Golding.

Tessa Paterson and her new pony Tommy, 1988. Tessa is pictured in Milton Avenue outside her parents' house. Tommy was liveried at John Vowles' stables in Sandford Road, Weston.

Community midwives, pictured at the new Weston General Hospital, 1987. They were moved there from the old 21-bed General Practitioner maternity unit at Ashcombe House at the top of The Drive.
Left to right: Kathleen Taylor, Faith Owen, Maureen Faragher, Debbie White, ?, Helen Harvey.

Community midwife Jane Paterson, weighing a newborn baby after a home delivery, 1983.

Clare Paterson of Walliscote Junior
School, Walliscote Grove Road, playing
hockey at Baytree Playing Field, c.1981.

Somerset Bowling Club members at Clarence Park Bowling Club, photographed with World Champion David Bryant,
1987. David Bryant began his career as a member of Clevedon Bowls Club. He went on to become World and
Commonwealth Champion Singles player and winner of countless national and international titles following his first
appearance for England in 1958.
Left to right, back row: ?, ?, Pauline Dunn, Dot Hunt; Front row, l-r: Jean Firrell, David Bryant, Hilda Goold, ?

The Mayor, Cllr James Dickson and Mrs Dickson with the Committee, inspecting prize vegetables at the Milton Baptist Church Flower Show, c.1981.

Richard Hopkins' Dance studio. The Thursday night dance class with their First Gold Bar examination awards for Ballroom (Modern) Dancing, 1985. Left to right, back row: Russell Mitton, David Harkness, Keith Cox, Sharon Poole (class helper, holding 4th Gold Star for Ballroom); front: Sue Mitton, Ada Harkness, Sue Smith (instructor), Mary Toogood.

The curatorial staff of Woodspring Museum, June 1987. This photograph was taken at the opening of Clara's Cottage next to the Museum in Burlington Street, Weston. Left to right: Sharon Poole (social historian), Sylvia Bingley (administration), Alec Coles (natural historian), Jane Evans (curator), Vicky Pirie (archaeologist).

Clara's Cottage Parlour, June 1987
The small terraced cottage was purchased by Woodspring District Council in 1985. Between 1901 and 1985 the cottage at no.13 Burlington Street, next door to what is currently North Somerset Museum, had been lived in by successive members of the Payne family. When Clara Payne lived there between 1901 and 1952, she brought in some extra money by letting out one room to visitors. When the Council bought the cottage, the aim was to restore it to how it looked at the turn of the nineteenth century and to recreate the three main rooms – lodger's bedroom, parlour and kitchen - using objects from the museum collections. The opening was performed by Hedli Nicklaus from the radio programme *The Archers*. Clara's Cottage is probably the most popular display in North Somerset Museum, but at the time of writing is sadly under threat of closure as plans have been revealed to close and sell the whole Burlington Street museum site and move some displays to a small section of the Winter Gardens. Local campaigners, including Clara's grand nephew, Brian Austin, are fighting against the move but only time will tell what the outcome will be.

The kitchen of Clara's Cottage. This is shown decorated for Christmas with holly on the clock on the mantelpiece and mince pies baking in the range oven. Again, nearly all the items were donated by local people or, like the range, came from North Somerset properties. The dresser was original to the cottage.

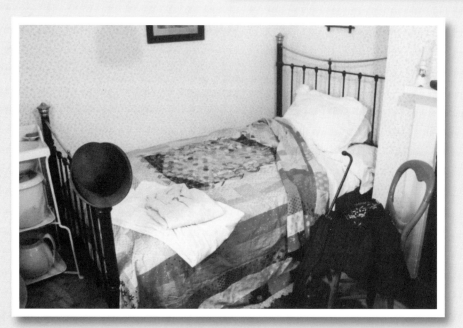

The lodger's bedroom in Clara's Cottage, complete with iron bedstead with feather mattress and patchwork quilt. All the items were donated by local people. Even the period congoleum flooring came from a cottage in Uphill.

The back yard of Clara's Cottage. Visitors to the Museum would walk through this yard to enter the cottage by the back door. A team of gardening volunteers led by Len Trowbridge (seen with his back to the camera), helped to turn the yard into a pretty garden.

The 1990s

By the 1990s, Weston had evolved into a very different town from that of previous decades, as economic and government pressures began to have a visible effect on the town. Hotels were closing in ever greater numbers as fewer people spent much longer than a weekend at UK resorts anymore, and self catering was increasingly popular instead. Many of the larger properties were even converted into bail hostels and drug rehabs and some hotels became residential and nursing homes for the elderly. Despite closures, there were corresponding openings too. Knightstone Baths closed for the final time but were replaced by Hutton Moor indoor pool and sports centre. In 1994 Birnbeck Pier was closed as unsafe, but the following year the new Sealife Centre opened. This was the first new seaside pier built in Britain for nearly 50 years. The Centre was opened on 7 June 1995 by BBC children's presenter, Michaela Strachan. It focused on the undersea world of the Bristol Channel with state-of-the-art aquaria including a 50,000 gallon tank with walk through tunnel.

There was other investment too. The new Sovereign Shopping Centre opened in 1992 and work began on a large new extension to the Winter Gardens. The old Starlight Room was demolished along with the tennis courts and a conference centre and additional meeting rooms built on the northern side. It was opened by HRH the Princess Royal on 21 January 1992. Housing estates were increasingly filling in the green spaces between Weston and its neighbouring villages – Locking, Worle, Wick St Lawrence and St Georges. There were also new transport links, with the dual carriageway link road to the motorway.

In 1996, another local government re-organisation abolished the unpopular and contrived County of Avon. A new unitary authority of North Somerset was established, using the same boundaries as the District of Woodspring.

The defining memory locally of this decade was the murder of local celebrity Jill Dando at her home in London on 26 April 1999 at the age of 37. It left the town in a state of shock similar to that generated by the death of Princess Diana 18 months previously. At Jill's funeral in May, the streets were lined with people wishing to pay their last respects as the cortege passed from the service at Clarence Road Baptist Church to the interment at Ebdon Road Cemetery in Worle.

"Weston Our Weston, A Tale of Wheels and Deals" was a musical show put on at Weston Playhouse in June 1992 to commemorate the 150th anniversary of Weston becoming a town. It starred some 59 local people of the 1990s, each playing local people of the 1840s. The original script was written by Brian Austin and was directed by Geoffrey Collins with Musical Direction by Brendan Ashe. The stage sets were by John Butler, lighting by Pete Magor, costumes by Mary Edbrooke and choreography by Eddie Mercer. Left to right: Hilary Semmens as Mrs Provis, ?, Ray Edbrook as William Cox, Mike Usher as Richard Parsley.

Another scene from "Weston Our Weston", 1992. Left to right: ?, Steve Dibben as Hugh Council, Alan Bowler, ? , Terry Brown as Isaac Council, ?, ?, Barbara Smith (in large bonnet), Brian Austin, ?, ?, Heather Collings.

Phil "Iron Man" Haskins with Weston Super Ted, 1994. Phil was well-known locally for his fund-raising activities and charity work, and especially for entering triathlons. He was a retired fire fighter and at the time of this photo worked in North Somerset Museum. This event was part of a fund-raising drive to raise sufficient money to purchase a Gainsborough oil painting of Wadham Pigott, Lord of the Manor and Rector of Weston-super-Mare, 1750 – 1823. Wadham was the first of the Lords of the Manor to make his home in Weston, at Grove House, rather than the family seat at Brockley Court. The painting was sold by the family in 1911 during a time of financial hardship. The appeal was successful and with a substantial grant from the National Art Collections Fund, the author Jeffrey Archer (who grew up in Weston and launched the appeal) and many local people, the painting returned home. The portrait can currently be seen in the Museum, together with the matching painting of Wadham's brother, John, which had remained in the family and was gifted to the Borough of Weston together with all the family portraits in 1947.

The Sovereign Centre development site, c.1990. This was probably the biggest building project in Weston for decades. It began with the demolition of existing properties in Salisbury Terrace and Royal Arcade in the late 1980s. This photograph was taken from the upper floors of the General Post Office just before it too was demolished for the scheme. The finished shopping centre finally opened in 1992.

Burton House School Old Girls reunion, 6 July 1999.
Left to right, back row: Joyce Wren (née Clout), Sheila Lockwood (née Payne), Joan Croft (née Rainey), Peggy Willcox (née Ellis), Ruth Smith (née Lane), Sylvia Cook (née White), Maureen Cockram (née Champion), Shirley Jones (née Tremlett), Valerie Haskins (née Faulkner), Susan Poole (née Davies); front row: Margaret Harvey (née Betteridge), Helen Rushton (née Gardner), Greta Keeling (née Gardner), Christine Gilbert (née Drew), Joan Player-Mason (née Smith).

Reunion of various cast members from the British Legion Pantomimes (see page 70). This was held at Dauncey's Hotel, Claremont Crescent, Weston, 11 February, 1995. Left to right: ?, ?, Brenda Hutchins, ?, Adrian Harper, Keith Dimolene, Ollie Pratlett, Jolene Alexander (Principal of the Alexander School of Dancing), Tony Hughes, Doris Wilsher (nee Foreman). At the piano is Jessica Hillman.

Leaving party for Clare Paterson held at the Cabot Hotel, before she left on a Gap Year trip to Australia, 1990. Pictured are some of her Saturday workmates from W.H.Smith and school friends from Churchill School. Fourth from left is Jonathan Dyer and to the right of him is Clare.

From left to right, Tessa, Clare and John Paterson, photographed at Woodspring Priory, Kewstoke in 1993.

The Uphill Hand-Bell Ringers performing in the courtyard of North Somerset Museum, Burlington Street, 1999. The open courtyard of this lovely building in Burlington Street has wonderful acoustics, and has been the venue for all sorts of musical entertainment from string quartets to folk groups, hand-bell ringers to Victorian music boxes.

The Weston fishing boat *Flare* is manoeuvred into North Somerset Museum, February 1990. This is a Weston Flatner, a type of local boat built with a flat bottom, so as to have a shallow draft and to stay upright on the beaches and mudflats at low tide. They were used along the Somerset coastline at Weston, Clevedon and Bridgwater. *Flare* was built at Kimbers Yard at Bridgwater for the local Payne family and was the last Weston Flatner ever built. She is clinker-built with overlapping planks of larch and was powered by a diesel engine, unlike the older flatners which were powered by sail, and was purchased for North Somerset Museum with a grant from the Science Museum Purchase Fund. Although originally built as fishing vessels, by the late nineteenth century, flatners were often used as pleasure craft in the summer, taking tourists on trips round the bay.

A New Millennium

Weston entered the new millennium with fewer amenities and attractions than it had fifty years previously. In the intervening years the town has lost its airport, regular steamer services, the open air swimming pool, Knightstone Theatre...the list could go on. Appreciation for the town's past appears to have been lost in the need to respond to the poor economic climate and changing holiday patterns. For example the Rozel Hotel was demolished for a new apartment block, as was Overcombe in the Shrubbery – one of the oldest residences left in Weston. However, Weston has continued to grow in other ways as new residential developments have covered the once-green fields at Locking Castle, Wick St Lawrence and St Georges. Notable new public buildings include the Silica, the new Court House at St Georges and the Campus at Locking Castle. The Silica was intended as a new piece of public art as well as providing a bus shelter and food stall in its base. It stands as a centrepiece in the improved pedestrianised area at the junctions of High Street, Regent Street and Meadow Street once known as Big Lamp Corner. The Campus is another example of a new multi-use building, combining Heron's Moor Primary School, Baytree Special School, a library, sports hall and meeting rooms.

In July 2001, Weston featured on the BBC *Ground Force* gardening programme, as the team defied torrential rain and a tropical storm, to build a garden in Grove Park, in memory of Jill Dando. This garden was built on the site of an old rose garden in front of Grove House and continues to be very popular with visitors today.

The local event of this decade was the fire on the Grand Pier, which destroyed the famous pavilion built in 1930. On 28 July 2008, many residents stood in stunned silence watching as what began as a small column of smoke from the north east tower, spread and raged through the whole pavilion until all that remained was a twisted metal skeleton. At the time of writing a new, larger and state-of-the-art Pavilion is being constructed, that will make the Grand Pier the best in the country, if not the world.

2007 also saw the start of the greatest engineering feat seen in Weston since the construction of the sea wall and promenade began in the 1880s. The new flood and tidal defence scheme involves building an additional splash wall on the road side of the widened promenade, and a stepped wave dispersion system at the base of the seawall below beach level. There will also be new surfacing, lighting, seating and artworks. Three years later work is continuing, but it will provide a rejuvenated and pedestrian-friendly sea front area to take Weston into the twenty-first century and beyond.

For four consecutive summers, Channel Four Television has staged T4 on the beach, and is due to return in 2010. This huge concert featuring top bands is held on a summer Sunday in July and has brought much needed revenue into the town.

These years of economic frugality might well help to regenerate British seaside resorts. The events in New York on 11 September 2001 and the consequent reluctance to fly abroad over the following few years has also aided the industry. Some six million visitors came to North Somerset in 2008/9 and tourism is still worth over £180 million to the district, employing nearly 5000 people. However, the last two years have seen the retail areas suffer from the unemployment and reduced disposable income the credit crunch has generated and many shops stand empty in the High Street and other retail areas.

Weston is changing, and will continue to change. Hopefully it will be for the better. We must wait and see.

Weston Carnival, 2007. This huge two-part articulated float was on the theme "Cossacks". Illuminated carnival processions began in Weston in 1889 with Weston Cycling Club members in fancy dress on bicycles and carrying lanterns. These developed into an annual event until the First World War in 1914. After the War Summer Carnivals became popular fundraisers for the St John's Ambulance Brigade. It was not until 1925 that winter ones were re-introduced alongside the summer ones, but once again, war intervened in 1939. The Summer Carnivals were reinstated in 1958. The November Carnivals did not return to Weston until the 1970s and are now closely linked to the Somerset Carnival Circuit that begins with the Guy Fawkes Carnival at Bridgwater and ends two weeks later at Weston. The Summer Carnivals died out in the 1980s, mainly due to the retirement of the main organisers, chief among whom was Mrs Gertrude Butters. Local Carnival Clubs start planning the next year's entry soon after each carnival. Fundraising events are held throughout the summer to raise sufficient money to build these amazing constructions. There is no charge to watch two hours of magic pass by. All contributions to the collectors are voluntary and people come from all over the country every November to see this amazing spectacle.

Weston Carnival, 2007. Another magnificent float, this time on the theme of Narnia from the books by C.S. Lewis.

Playhouse staff, October 2003. For this show, entitled *Something Else*, Brian Austin brought together a mix of local talent for a traditional variety performance at Weston Playhouse. It was written by Brian as a personal tribute to the fondly remembered summer shows that used to appear at Knightstone Theatre.   Left to right, back: Pete Tivey, Pete Magor, Colin Tyler, Dave Clothier, Norman Trenner; Front: Brian Austin, Sian Cross.

Seafront improvements, 2007-2010. High tides and westerly gales have often resulted in waves crashing over the sea wall and flooding seafront properties. Major damage was caused in 1903 and 1981, when the sea wall was breached and the Marine Lake colonnade wrecked. Global warming and rising sea levels predict this will happen more often and so in June 2007 work began on the new flood defence scheme. Paid for by a £12m grant from DEFRA, the 1888 sea wall was strengthened, with concrete "steps" laid below the sand at the base to dissipate the strength of the waves. The promenade was widened and a second "splash" wall built alongside the road to contain any water that might come over the sea wall. This will then drain back out to sea. At the same time a £1.2m grant from the South West Regional Development Agency's Civic Pride Initiative is providing for improved seating, lighting, surfacing and street furniture. Work is still underway but it should look magnificent when it is completed.

The Grand Pier fire, 28 July 2009. The fire that destroyed the Grand Pier Pavilion is probably the most memorable event of the decade in Weston. What began, early on a Monday morning, as a small column of smoke in the north east tower, rapidly spread so that within about half an hour, the 1930 art deco pavilion was lost. The column of black smoke could clearly be seen across the Channel in Wales. Local people stood by roadsides in disbelief as a much loved and familiar landmark dissolved into a tangle of twisted metal and charred wood. The owners, brother and sister Kerry and Michelle Michael, had only owned the pier for around six months, having bought it from the Brenner family who had owned and run it for the last sixty years. However the Michaels lost no time and vowed to build a bigger and better pavilion. This is now well under construction, as can be seen in the second photograph, and is estimated to open in June 2010.

Sand Sculpture Exhibition on the Beach Lawns, 3 August 2006. A prophetic image as the Grand Pier Pavilion seen here clutched in the hands of King Kong, was indeed destroyed just two years later, only by fire rather than a giant ape! Sand sculpture was a popular seaside attraction in British resorts around the turn of the twentieth century. Then it was patriotic scenes from the Boer War that drew admiring glances. Nowadays it has been revived as a world-wide competitive skill. There is even a World Sand Sculpting Academy based in Holland. The right kind of sand is important, and Weston beach sand is perfect. The first display of Sand Sculpture in Weston in recent years was in 2005. Proving popular with visitors, the following year's display was bigger and better and it is now an annual festival. This sculpture of King Kong was created by Joris and Jaap, two Dutchmen. It stood 10 feet tall and took 20 tonnes of sand to construct. Each year has a set theme – Fairytales in 2007, the Seven Continents in 2008 and Creatures of the Deep in 2009. One of the 2007 sculptors went on to win a gold medal at the World Championships in Canada.

Violet Hookins at a reunion of Burton House School pupils and staff, July 2003. Violet first went to the school as a pupil in 1921. Immediately upon leaving, she took up a post teaching mathematics there. Miss Hookins died in December 2004 aged 94.

Sportsmen's Lunch, held at the Winter Gardens, to celebrate the centenary of Clarence Park Bowling Club, April 2007.
Left to right: Trevor Ward (Vice President of Clarence Park Bowling Club), Bob Cornwall (Vice Captain of Clarence Park Bowling Club), David Rhys-Jones (BBC Broadcaster), Brian Rose (Director of Cricket at Somerset County Cricket Club and ex-pupil of Weston-super-Mare Grammar School), Derek Stevens (President of Clarence Park Bowling Club), John Durston (Hon. Secretary of Somerset Bowling Association), Paula Howell (Mayor of Weston-super-Mare), Richard Howell, Ron Higgins (Clarence Park Bowling Club member), Nigel Oldfield (Chief Executive of the World Bowls Tour), Alan Richardson (Match Secretary, Clarence Park Bowling Club).

Chris Roberts at the Old Westonians' Reunion, 2009. Chris is standing next to a watercolour painting entitled "Wings over Weston Grammar, 1958" by Clive Irvine-Gizzie of the Frome Society of Disabled Artists. The painting was one of the raffle prizes at the reunion lunch and was based on a photograph taken by Chris Roberts, who gained his pilot's licence soon after leaving school in 1954.

Reunion of Old Westonians, 4 October 2009. Around 170 ex-pupils of the former Weston Boys' and Girls' Grammar Schools gathered at the Royal Hotel, to reminisce about the time they were at school together over 50 years ago! The school originally opened in 1922 as The County School, in Nithsdale Road. It moved from that site to a new purpose-built school in Broadoak Road in 1935, which, ten years later, became Weston Grammar School. The Boys and Girls were strictly segregated at this period. In 1971 the Grammar Schools were merged with Uphill Secondary Modern School to form Broadoak Comprehensive School. The Uphill site became the Sixth Form Centre, and the Broadoak Road site the main school. In 1999 the old school buildings were demolished and Broadoak Community School was built, specialising in mathematics & computing.

Several of those at the reunion were at school as far back as the 1930s, among them Mary Griffiths (née Rainbow) and Martin Davies. Some were there during the years of the Second World War, when evacuees from London schools shared the buildings. Others present at the reunion attended the schools in the 1950s and early 1960s, and have memories of rationing and other post-war hardships. While the majority of the attendees still live in the Somerset area, others travelled from as far afield as Canada, the USA and Australia.

Former pupils Alison Finney, Jeff Hynds and Bryan Claxton organise the annual reunions. Left to right, back row: ?, ?, Doris Wilsher (née Foreman), ?, Roy Hicks, Brian Pike, ?, Alan White, John Campkin, Peter Rainbow, Les Brook, ?, Mary Griffiths (née Rainbow); front: Jean Holden, Greta Gee (née Guest), Jane Johnstone (née Hunt), ?, Tryphena Campkin, Barbara Green.